Dr Meg

MEG PATTERSON

An Autobiography

WORD PUBLISHING
Nelson Word Ltd
Milton Keynes, England
WORD AUSTRALIA
Kilsyth, Australia
WORD COMMUNICATIONS LTD
Vancouver, B.C., Canada
STRUIK CHRISTIAN BOOKS (PTY) LTD
Cape Town, South Africa
JOINT DISTRIBUTORS SINGAPORE –
ALBY COMMERCIAL ENTERPRISES PTE LTD
and
CAMPUS CRUSADE, ASIA LTD
PHILIPPINE CAMPUS CRUSADE FOR CHRIST
Quezon City, Philippines
CHRISTIAN MARKETING NEW ZEALAND LTD
Havelock North, New Zealand
JENSCO LTD
Hong Kong
SALVATION BOOK CENTRE
Malaysia

DR MEG

I would like to dedicate this book to those who have made my life so wonderful: to my husband, George; to my children and grandchildren.

Nothing will ever be attempted if all possible objections must first be overcome.

Samuel Johnson

Since my youth, O God, you have taught me,
    and to this day I declare your marvellous deeds:
Even when I am old and grey,
    do not forsake me, O God,
till I declare your power to the next generation,
    your might to all who are to come.

Psalm 71:17–18 (NIV)

CONTENTS

*Meg, aged seven, outside the family home
in Stanley Street, Aberdeen, Scotland.
1930*

- 1 -

Finding My Goal in Surgery and in India

$\mathcal{A}$berdeen, in the north-east of Scotland, in 1922 was a small and busy fishing and farming city, with a notable university, before it became famous in the 1970s as 'the oil capital of Britain'. On market days the strong brogue of the fishermen mingled with the quieter, lilting tones of the Deeside farmers, softening the otherwise harsh impression which the distinctively grey quarried rock of the buildings and houses made on the visitor.

I was brought up in a three-storey, terraced house in Stanley Street, a short distance from Union Street, the main shopping centre of the city. My father, Alex Ingram, was a railway official, and able to live in comfortable circumstances. I was the youngest of five children, two sons and three daughters—Charles, Edith, Alice, Edward and myself.

I was a fairly solitary child, mostly by personal preference. I was perfectly happy to be on my own, whether in the home, at school, or at play. My closest companion in the family was Ed, who was three years older than me. There were fourteen years between me and my oldest brother Charlie, and the others had lots of friends of their own ages. This meant that our house was filled with male and female visitors as our parents kept an open and hospitable home.

When I was seven years old I got a bicycle like the other members of the family, and cycling outings with Ed and friends was always a great pleasure. Later I cycled to university, which was some distance away from our family home.

But my most enjoyable childhood memories are of our annual holidays. My father's position in the railways meant we had a month's holiday and free first-class travel for the family, and every year we travelled to some new place in England. He always selected a farm, close to the sea, and I can still recall almost every one of the trips—especially riding the farm horses, or the tractors, and helping to look after the young animals.

Ours was a home where Christian values were taught and discussed at daily devotional readings of the Bible. We had prayers and reading in the morning, a reading from Proverbs at lunch, and singing, Bible study and prayer after dinner. My father was a leading figure among the Christian groups known as Plymouth Brethren, and outside his working hours his time was spent at Bible study meetings, or preaching at household meetings throughout the Highlands of Scotland. A close friend of his was Peter Bruce, the father of Professor F. F. Bruce, the noted Bible scholar, and together they preached at hundreds of these gatherings for many years in Highland villages and towns.

'Plymouth Brethren', as they were called, were not really from Plymouth, nor wholly composed of brothers. They were one of many groups who throughout ecclesiastical history had broken away from a sterile religious traditionalism in an attempt to get back to Scriptural simplicity of worship. In the nineteenth century they emerged in Britain from Ireland, and only later came to Plymouth in the south of England, which gave them their distinctive name. They believed in the priesthood of all believers, had no ordained pastors in charge of their churches, and they called each other 'brother' and 'sister'. Hence the name. They had many distinguished preachers, teachers, scholars and writers, and their influence in evangelical Christian circles in Britain, Europe and elsewhere extended well beyond the numbers they represented.

I mention this because the Plymouth Brethren were very influential in Scotland in the early part of the twentieth century, particularly among the fishermen of the north-east and the miners of central Scotland, and it was in this community that I was brought up. My father went to Holborn Gospel Hall, one of the Brethren meeting-places in Aberdeen, and took us with him several times a week. However, when I was eleven years of age and wanted to be baptised by immersion in the customary Brethren fashion, the strict elders of Holborn Hall refused for reasons that were never explained to me; my father accepted their decision, so I went to the more 'open assembly'—as the Brethren called their more permissive church gatherings— of Hebron Hall, with my sister Edith.

I was educated at Aberdeen Central School—now Aberdeen Academy—and finished my studies there in 1939, having been Dux of the Year, or leading scholar, four times. I was still only sixteen at the time, but was accepted for Aberdeen University to read medicine, and graduated MB,ChB when I was twenty-one, one of the youngest women doctors ever to do so, I was told. I was also awarded the First Prize in Surgery.

While at university I was very actively involved with the InterVarsity Fellowship, in both their evangelical and fellowship activities, which increased my circle of friends tremendously. About this same time the Second World War began and this brought a flow of visiting servicemen to our church and home. Some of these were relatives, especially from Canada, and with their help I learned to ice-skate and in return took them to swim in early morning dips in the North Sea dawn—lit by Aberdeen's famous 'northern lights'. In summer weather we went mountain walking and climbing in the glorious scenery of the nearby hills and rivers of Benachie and Deeside.

Meg in the back garden of her Aberdeen home, after graduating as a doctor at the age of twenty-one. 1944

I went to work in the Royal Hospital for Sick Children for a year, where I discovered that children made wonderful patients. In those days we gave children heroin instead of morphine for post-operative pain and I was curious as to what brought such peace to screaming suffering little ones, so I got the nurses to give me a shot. I was violently sick. Little did I realise then that I may have escaped the risk of becoming an addict because of this reaction!

For the next six months I was a house-surgeon in the highly regarded Aberdeen Maternity Hospital, before going to St James Hospital in Balham, London, to work as Registrar under Mr Norman Tanner, the world-famous surgeon in the oesophageal, gastric and intestinal fields.

This was a unique opportunity, for not only was I a

young woman in what was widely regarded as a man's field (the few women who went into surgery usually restricted their interests to obstetrics and gynaecology) but working with Norman Tanner, who was internationally admired for his superb surgery, was a choice appointment; also, it was during the Second World War when there were so many operations to be done by so few staff that there were unparalleled opportunities to develop surgical skills.

I had wanted to be a surgeon for as long as I could remember. It was not so much the technical expertise which fascinated me, although I never ceased to marvel at Norman Tanner's brilliant surgical techniques, but the rapidity with which surgical intervention could transform a person from near death to healthy life, releasing the crippled into mobility, and the physically captive into a joyous freedom.

A female colleague, Martha, an anaesthetist from South Ireland, and I were the only two young doctors in the hospital. Several of the other, older, doctors had just been discharged from the services as the war was ending, and they viewed Martha and me, despite our considerable academic experience, with amused tolerance. One of the senior surgeons, Des, who was in charge of emergency surgery, taught me important practical surgical procedures, and was astonished to learn, in the occasional breaks between operations, that Martha and I had practically no knowledge of sexual matters; that it had never been taught in Medical School, and of course was never mentioned in Brethren circles. So, on our nights on duty, on the rare occasions when we had some time for tea and a chat, Des would educate us on the 'facts of life'! During my eighteen months there I reckon I had an average of three hours' sleep a night. But although the work was so demanding, it was also rewarding in terms of friendship between the doctors.

Because of the concentrated experience I had obtained working with Norman Tanner I decided to try for the prestigious Fellowship of the Royal College of Surgeons in

Edinburgh University much sooner than most aspiring surgeons. I took a short, five-month cram course together with my brother Ed, who had just been demobbed from the army. I was the only woman applicant for this course from among ninety-nine male surgeons, but despite this—or perhaps, because of it!—I thoroughly enjoyed the experience. I was successful at the first attempt, and so at twenty-five years of age I could add the highly prized degree of FRCS (Edin.) after my name. Later, I was to learn officially from the College that I was one of only twenty women who obtained the FRCSE before 1950, and I heard that most of these went into the field of gynaecology.

It was 1948, and the Second World War was finished. I was now equipped by academic and hospital experience to work anywhere in the country, with a highly promising career ahead of me. But I was strangely very uncertain and unhappy about following that admittedly attractive course.

From the age of sixteen, when my much-loved mother had died, I had been totally occupied with academic studies of one kind or another. The intervening six years of war had brought an exciting new dimension into our family life, for in addition to our own relatives who were in the forces we had always kept an open home and entertained widely. However, these were mostly Christians, and the matters of mutual interest were usually very circumscribed. Because of the unusual war circumstances it was easier to meet, and 'date', eligible young men, which was normally discouraged in Brethren circles unless it was 'serious'. I had been dated by several of these passing visitors, but with no developing interest. Consequently, my knowledge of the world outside the very limited circle of Brethren acquaintances, and Christian activities, was extremely restricted.

At university I had been a member of the evangelical InterVarsity Fellowship, and, later, the Christian Medical Fellowship. Both of these Christian organisations, and the Plymouth Brethren, had a strong missionary influence, and it was this combination of circumstances that was now warring with my secular ambitions on completing my Fellowship. I had no great personal desire to be a foreign missionary, but on the other hand, neither had I any great driving ambition simply to be a self-centred career woman. I did know that I wanted something meaningful, something challenging, in which I could use the skills God had given me.

A few days after my Fellowship in Surgery was confirmed, I went off for a holiday with a girl friend, to think over my future free of distractions. But I returned to London, still undecided. It was July, 1948, and a warm, sunny day. I thought I would go to see a film—for only the second time in my life. While living in Edinburgh, my brother Ed and I had gone to see our first film, *Gone with the Wind*. Films, together with music and dancing, were frowned on among Brethren as 'worldly pleasures', and even going to see a 'good' film or attend a concert could engender a considerable amount of guilt.

But while I was still on the subway on the way to the cinema I was startled to hear a voice saying to me, 'Go to Bristol.' It was so unexpected and unusual—I had never had such an experience of hearing a 'spiritual voice' before, although I had heard and read of others who had—that it confused me. Why Bristol?

As it happened, my sister Alice lived in Bristol with her husband Willie, and their small sons, Angus and Colin. I had made no plans to visit them, but the direction had been so clear and definite that I stopped my journey, went straight to the railway station, and bought a ticket for Bristol.

When I arrived at Alice's house I found that she had been in bed very sick for three days with what her doctor had diagnosed as 'diarrhoea and vomiting'. But, when I examined her, I discovered she had acute appendicitis, and perhaps early peritonitis. I telephoned my concern to her doctor, who arranged for her to be operated on right away.

At the hospital the surgeon who was to do the operation was a Mr Melville Capper, well known in Christian medical circles; and after the operation was finished, as we talked, he invited me to an InterVarsity Fellowship Conference being held near Bristol the following day.

I went there with him as his guest, and during the conference he introduced me to one of the speakers, Professor Rendle Short, a noted Professor of Surgery and an outstanding Christian. Professor Short was brusque in manner, but very interested to hear of my Fellowship—and age!—and present indecision about career. Without any hesitation he said I must consider going to India, to Ludhiana Christian Medical College.

The Medical College, in the Punjab province of northern India, had been an all-women's hospital and college until the mass killings between Hindus and Muslims, following on Indian independence the previous year, had forced a change in policy. The Principal, a woman surgeon, had died suddenly, and as she was the only general surgeon, the Indian Government was considering closing down the college and hospital for lack of a qualified resident surgeon-tutor. Professor Short was suggesting that I take her place.

It was the answer to my prayer, and I agreed to go as soon as possible. For the next few months my life was a mad rush of preparations, farewells and public meetings, and I finally left England for India by ship in December, 1948. The journey to Bombay took three weeks, with several visits to ports en route, and the fascination of foreign places rapidly wiped out thoughts of home.

From the time I arrived in Bombay—overwhelmed by the noise, the crowds, the bustle, the chaos, the smells, and then the seemingly endless train journey over hundreds of miles of parched plains, but with breathtakingly beautiful scenes and friendly people—I became absorbed with the country. It was not just a new place, a new culture, a new way of life; it was a whole new experience. It was only a year since India had gained her independence, and there were still signs of the old British Imperial Raj everywhere in evidence. On the trains white-clothed and turbaned waiters served the most delicious curries with courtesy and consideration, while the railway system worked with astonishing efficiency amidst the surrounding apparent chaos. But then the murderous Hindu–Muslim race riots had begun when independence was attained and there were signs of this everywhere, too.

I loved Ludhiana, near the bloody border between India and Pakistan, scene of some of the worst fighting. In the months prior to my arrival long train-loads of wounded and dying men and women were brought into Ludhiana and had been left lying in the railway sidings awaiting attention, or death. The hospital was overcrowded, understaffed and poorly equipped—the patients spilling out of the packed wards into the open verandahs on wooden charpoys for beds. A black cloud of flies would arise from their recumbent bodies when anyone approached.

The Christian Medical Hospital had not been planned as such, but had just grown as a collection of buildings on either side of the main road of the town, next to the sprawling American Presbyterian Mission compound. The college staff and student residences were on one side of the road, and the hospital buildings on the other. The operating theatre was simply, even primitively, equipped, not even having an anaesthetic machine when I arrived; all operations had to be done using cotton masks and dripped ether or chloroform. A few surgical instruments were good, but very old-fashioned. There was very little money available for equipment—or for salaries—and that had made it difficult to get quality staff. I was being paid two hundred rupees a month (at that time worth about £20 sterling), out of which I had to pay for food and an ayah to clean my bedsitting room.

The surgery I had to perform was often dramatic. I had become accustomed to challenging surgical operations while in London, but there I was surrounded by experts to approach for advice, and could use the latest in surgical instruments. In Ludhiana I was virtually on my own, with minimum equipment, and patients in conditions beyond any experience in the West. By the time they reached me in a desperate and often moribund state they had perhaps been to several doctors, or quacks of various kinds, in order to avoid operations. Amputations of limbs, often grossly gangrenous, were common.

One patient was a Sikh factory worker. It is the custom for Sikh men to keep their hair long, wound in a top-knot, and secured under a tightly rolled turban. A month before this man had had his hair caught in a machine, and his entire scalp—including one ear and one eyebrow—had been ripped off. The bare skull bone was a mass of pus. I knew that no ordinary skin graft would 'take' under such conditions, so over several weeks I applied pinch-grafts (tiny pieces of skin taken mostly from his thighs) every few days until his head was completely covered with skin. He did not mind his bizarrely scarred appearance, because the scarred area of his head was covered with his turban.

On another occasion I was called to a mission station some forty miles away where their Indian doctor had had an accident on his motorcycle. One knee had been almost completely severed, except, fortunately, for the large nerves and blood-vessels at the back of the knee. I had had no formal training in orthopaedic surgery, and sewing together the complex ligaments of the knee, knowing that any mistake would destroy its usefulness, was a tense experience. But he recovered well enough to walk and ride his motor-cycle again.

I also had to perform gynaecological operations when I was called to the surrounding mission hospitals, and again I had no training in this field. I joked with the nurses that they should boil up the gynaecological textbook together with the instruments so that I could read it as I operated. Often in these operations there were only three of us in the operating theatre—the patient, the nursing Sister and me. I would give the patient a spinal anaesthetic while the Sister prepared the table of theatre linen and instruments for the operation. Both of us would then 'scrub up' to do the operations—and I prayed that the patient's blood pressure would not fall as a result of the anaesthetic, because there was no one there to measure it.

All the Christian staff, both British and Indian, were assigned groups of students for once-weekly recreational evenings, which were held in our own rooms. All the students participated, although about half of them were either Hindu or Sikh, and many from Christian backgrounds were only nominal in their inherited beliefs. These evenings usually ended with a Bible study of various subjects, and they often produced close and lasting friendships as well as conversions. Those who were converted usually had a hard time from their families, on occasions even being banished from home, and many developed into fine Christians.

I thoroughly enjoyed my work, hectic though it was. I was the only resident general surgeon, and was responsible for all the surgery previously performed by visiting specialists of various kinds—when they were available. There were about six hundred students to be taught, mostly female, with only four males when I first arrived. The first male resident orthopaedic surgeon, Bill Virgin from Canada, came soon after I did; followed by Stuart Bergsma of the United States of America, then others.

Language study, surgery and anatomy lectures for my classes, Bible studies for Scripture groups, crammed operating lists of all kinds of surgery, filled my days and nights. My life was as full of interest, challenge, excitement, responsibility, friendship and kindness as I could have wished.

I got a bicycle, and rode everywhere around Ludhiana. The hospital had a great reputation among the people, the bearded and turbaned martial Sikhs of the Punjab, and I was welcomed wherever I went. I would sit in the houses of patients or relatives or friends in my free time, or in the back rooms of their shops in the bazaars, chatting with them for hours, drinking the sweet mint tea or eating the delicious curries and sweetmeats.

It was a source of great interest and amusement that I was known professionally as 'Miss Ingram'. I could explain as much as I liked how in Britain, once a person graduated MB,ChB as the first medical degree, one became known as 'Doctor'. Then, if the individual went on to graduate in surgery, as I had done, the proper professional method of address was not 'Doctor' any more, but 'Mr' for men, and 'Miss' for women. To confuse the situation even more, I looked so young that I was often mistaken for a medical student. At some point, to avoid embarrassing confusion or stiff formality, I became known as 'Doctor Meg', and the name stuck.

Meg's first graduating class at Ludhiana Christian Medical College, Punjab, India. A few of the teaching staff are in the second row—Meg is next to Dame Edith Brown (in black dress), the founder of the college.
1950

I was rather amused to learn one of the reactions of the students. I had always thought I was gentle and tolerant in character, like my mother, but after my first group of students graduated as doctors, when we all got together to celebrate, they informed me that they were all terrified of me as a teacher. When I told my family about this later, they said, 'Why are you so surprised? Don't you know there is steel beneath that gentle surface?'! Actually, it was from this first group that one of the students, Mary Matthews (who was so brilliant that I usually had to mark her papers 100%), some years later was to become Medical Superintendent of the hospital.

The only real breaks in our busy lives were when we got out of the 110- to 120-degree heat of the plains and travelled up to the cool hill stations of Landour or Mussoorie, in the foothills of the Himalayan mountains. It had become an accepted practice for all foreigners living in India to go to hill stations in the midsummer monsoon season each year, either for vacations to recuperate or for language studies and examinations. It was also the occasion for rapid courtships and quick marriages.

In those years the preponderance of young women missionaries over men was in the ratio of four to one, and as most of the men were either married or engaged this left very few eligible males for the often homesick, lonely young women working in isolated mission compounds in a strange country. Stories of the various amatory encounters were often amusing, sometimes hilarious, occasionally incredible, but mostly sad.

One of my colleagues set her heart on finding a husband, and chose one who was already committed to someone else. However, nothing daunted, she requested prayer-support to change his mind and affections to her at the weekly missionary prayer meeting in the women's hostel. Not content to leave it to God she then sought out the man and told him of her conviction—to his surprise and consternation. Under pressure he agreed to pray about it, although he pointed out to her that he was due to leave the hill station the following morning. My colleague said that she would meet him at the bus station to hear his decision, and when she turned up, the man said it was indeed God's will for him to change to my colleague.

When she returned to Ludhiana she promptly asked for 'compassionate leave' for a month before her wedding; because, she said, as her new fiancé was almost forty years of age she would have to prepare herself for the physically demanding time facing her in the consummation of their union in the short time left to them! The amusing postscript was that they had four children in the next four years—and she wrote to me asking how she could stop them coming!

My own life, although filled with study and work, as mentioned earlier, had not entirely eliminated time for boy-friends. None of them, however, were important enough to interfere with my work. In Ludhiana the hospital and college staff were mostly women, except for the recent arrivals who were all married. But in the hill stations, as a surgeon with a growing reputation and a focus of some attention, I found myself with time—and inclination—to pursue this hitherto neglected interest. To be honest, if not entirely modest, I was in the unusual situation of being pursued rather than pursuing. Unfortunately, like my less fortunate missionary sisters, the ones who interested me were either married or engaged, the ones available I rejected without regret; and so each year I left the hill stations for the hospital uncommitted and unwon, but happy. I always had the memory of an occasion, shortly after my arrival in Ludhiana when I was thanking God for providing me with 'my life's work', and His reply was, 'If I tell you to leave here tomorrow, you will go.' What was important was that I knew I was doing what God wanted me to do, where He wanted me to be for the present.

- 2 -

Falling in Love in Kalimpong

*T*hree years after my arrival in India, in 1952, I arranged with two missionary friends—Muriel Clemenger, a pharmacist, and Betty Scrimgeour, a nurse—to go to a different hill station, to Kalimpong, twelve hundred miles away from Ludhiana, on the borders of Tibet, Bhutan, Sikkim and Nepal. Muriel had travelled to India on the same ship as a missionary returning to India, Molly McCabe, whose husband, George, was the farm manager of a Church of Scotland school and orphanage in Kalimpong, Dr Graham's Homes. I was invited to come for a holiday to Kalimpong with Muriel and Betty.

I was very excited at the prospect, for Tibet, a legendary country at any time, had been prominently in the news for the previous two years ever since the Chinese Communist army had invaded the country. Kalimpong was the end, or the beginning, of the six-month-long main trade route across Tibet to and from China, where the colourful caravans of the Tibetan muleteers bought and sold their goods. It was also the place where the wealthy Tibetan officials and aristocrats made their homes after escaping from the encroaching Chinese, and where the Indian newspapers claimed there was 'a nest of spies' infiltrating the neighbouring Himalayan countries.

After a long train journey across the plains of eastern India to the railhead township of Siliguri in north-east Bengal, we went by ancient taxi fifty miles up the most spectacular mountain road I had ever seen. The zig-zag bends wound through great forests and plunging canyons, with indescribably beautiful wild orchids hanging from the dense greens of the trees, and brilliantly coloured butterflies dazzlingly illuminating the sun-dappled shade.

Dr Graham's Homes was on a high ridge known as Deolo, to the north of Kalimpong itself, over four thousand feet above sea level, and looking out dramatically on the mighty 28,000-foot Kanchenjunga mountain range. The McCabes' home was on the far side of the Homes, perched on a flat shelf looking downwards into the valley and upwards along one of the side trails leading to distant Tibet.

Molly and George McCabe made me feel at home right away. They came from Scotland—George from Edinburgh, and Molly from Falkirk—about a hundred miles from my home town of Aberdeen. It was a very large, roomy farmhouse, and they said they had another Scot living with them, who was writing a book that Molly was typing, and we would meet at dinner.

When we had washed and changed I was ready for dinner, for it had been a long day of travel and the appetising smells coming from the kitchen were overwhelming. I was glad when Molly said they would not wait for the other guest.

We had only just begun to eat when the door opened and the guest came in, apologising for being late. George told him not to worry, and Molly announced with a flamboyant flourish: 'Ladies, this is Patterson of Tibet.' To my astonishment, without a smile, he inclined his head and with an exaggerated bow said: 'I'm pleased to have you meet me.'

He was slim, with a deep tan and full beard, very good-looking with regular features, grey-blue eyes under long eyebrows, and with browny-auburn hair falling in loose waves to his shoulders. Slightly above average height, he was dressed in a good-quality, well-cut sports jacket and flannels, and a colourful bow tie.

George and Molly had laughed at his response, and then introduced him to us individually, which he acknowledged with a slight nod. He sat next to me, and I wondered what it was going to be like for the next few weeks. Surely he couldn't be serious with that arrogant statement; no one could be that pompous. But he made no effort to alter that first impression. He said very little to me, or Muriel or Betty, although he was obviously on very good terms with George and Molly and conversed easily with them.

I had heard of George Patterson before, through mutual friends in Scotland, and had been friendly with one of his friends in northern India, John Mackie, who, like George Patterson in Tibet, had been a pioneer missionary in Afghanistan, both independent but associated with the Brethren. I had almost met him before I left Britain when I had been talking with some friends of mine who, unknown to me, were waiting for him to arrive. I was also aware of the wide publicity which the newspapers had given him over his three-year stay in Tibet, and his journey across Tibet from China by a route before then considered impossible. It was this publicity which Molly had been gently satirising in introducing him as she did, and which he had apparently taken seriously in acknowledging in his absurdly pompous manner. I was determined he would get no idolising from me, and if he didn't initiate a conversation I made no attempt to do so.

It did not affect the general atmosphere because he was rarely in the house except for the late meal, leaving immediately after breakfast, and after dinner retiring to his room to work on his book. At dinner he and George and Molly always had plenty to discuss together, and we visitors had lots to talk about regarding our holiday activities.

Kalimpong was a fascinating place, and it was no wonder that it received the wide publicity it did at the time. In addition to its spectacular setting, its single main street and network of side-streets were packed with milling crowds of various peoples from the nearby Himalayan countries, and from other parts of the world. Tall, powerfully built Khamba traders and muleteers from East Tibet, with yak-skin gowns and silver sword scabbards; slim, aristocratic officials from the closed cities of Central Tibet, with colourful silk robes and long jade earrings; small but deadly Gurkhas from Nepal, with white jackets and jodhpurs, carrying their menacingly curved *kukris*; stout and voluble Indian merchants, with Congress caps and white dhotis as trousers; squat Bhutanese in striped, knee-length kilted dress; and Sikkimese, Lepchas, Sikhs, Chinese and white Europeans of all kinds, shapes and sizes in their own distinctive dress.

The shops lining the busy streets were stacked with goods from China, Central Asia and overseas. Trucks from the plains of India plied the roads to supply the traders; and long lines of varied caravans of mules with tinkling neck-bells plodded in from the mountain trails of Tibet. The caravans were very colourful as the mules had their manes and tails plaited with woollen ribbons, the muleteers had coloured silks woven into their long hair, and the trader-owners had beautiful saddle-rugs on their horses.

The only hotel in Kalimpong was the Himalayan Hotel, owned by David 'Daddy' Macdonald, a Scot-Tibetan with close family ties to Tibet, whose three daughters—Annie, Vicky and Vera—ran the hotel as the centre of local social activities. It was only a small hotel, with about a dozen rooms, but it was constantly filled with world-famous media journalists, foreign diplomats, Indian Government and military officials, international scholars and jet-setters, writers, tourists and spies. At any time of the day, but especially in the evenings, the leading Tibetan officials would be entertained there by one or other of these groups seeking information on their chosen interests; or their younger sons and daughters, educated in Western-type schools and customs, would be in the lounge partying or dancing with the media people.

This was the milieu in which George Patterson moved, and with which his name was associated in scandalised gossip among the missionary community in Kalimpong. He was one of the very few people outside Tibet who could speak the language fluently, and he was in constant demand as an interpreter for official, media and social functions. According to the shocked women missionaries of Kalimpong he was the chosen escort of sensation-seeking jet-setters, famous media journalists and photographers, embassy secretaries, Bhutanese princesses, Indian film stars, Tibetan aristocrats, Sikkimese and Nepalese beauties—but, rarely, if ever, seen with a Christian woman missionary. He also played centre-forward with a leading local football team and his weekly exploits at the hugely attended games were a constant source of admiring or condemnatory comment. It was concluded that all the attention had gone to his head and he was now a 'backslider' as far as his former missionary work was concerned.

We had been three weeks with the McCabes, and I had scarcely spoken more than a few polite phrases with George Patterson (or 'Pat-la' as he was known to Tibetans and others in Kalimpong, and to distinguish him from George McCabe). I was puzzled by the contradictions between his attitudes with the McCabes—with whom he was relaxed and funny, self-mocking and natural—and the distant flippancy and cynicism which he displayed towards others. I wanted to discuss this dichotomy with him, but not strongly enough to attempt to cross the barrier of his silence.

It might never have gone beyond this mild interest if I had not been making polite conversation with him after breakfast, while waiting for my friends to come and join me. I casually asked him what he did all day when he was away from the house, and after a slight hesitation he said that he was working with a friend investigating Tibetan demonism. I was suddenly very interested and began bombarding him with questions about it, and discovered that the friend was Prince Peter of Greece and Denmark—cousin of Britain's Prince Philip—who was the leader of a Danish anthropological expedition to Central Asia, at that time living in Kalimpong. Prince Peter's wife, Princess Irene, was interested in parapsychology, and his mother, Princess Marie Bonaparte, was a lifetime confidante of Sigmund Freud and interested in psychic phenomena. The Tibetan under study was an 'oracle-priest', who was able to make contact with nine different Tibetan deities in trance-possession, and he was being filmed while under possession and in contact with these different deities.

This conversation broke down the polite and distant barrier between us, and I spent more time talking with him in the evenings after dinner, and in the mornings before he left. I found, as I had suspected, that he was quite different from what he showed earlier, and that he had read widely, thought deeply, experienced a great deal—and wanted to know much more. I found him intriguing.

When I returned one day from a very frustrating ride on one of the farm horses, which had refused to go further up the trail and stubbornly returned to the farm stables, I found George sitting at a table in the garden, grinning. It appeared he had been sitting there correcting his manuscript and, looking up, had seen the figure on the horse having trouble with it. At first he had thought it was Muriel, who had a reputation as an excellent horsewoman (and with whom, he informed me, Molly was determined to match him) and he was wickedly pleased at the rider's conspicuous difficulties.

I made no pretence at being able to ride so there was no pleasure, wicked or otherwise, to be derived from me, and he offered to take me out the next day and show me what to do. I agreed, and when we came to the same part of the trail where my horse had balked the day before, George gave it a sharp cut with his whip and it leapt away up the mountain trail. It kept going after that, and each time George tried to come alongside me on the narrow trail it pulled away ahead of him. It was now galloping, which I found much easier than the jolting canter, and I was enjoying myself when the trail narrowed suddenly and became very stony and rough. Again, George tried to come alongside me to catch the reins and slow it down, but it swerved sharply to the left up a side trail and I was thrown over its head, my own head just missing a large concrete water-block by an inch.

When I sat up there was no sign of George or the horses. By the time he appeared I was furious, for it had been frightening and I could have been killed—and it looked as if he couldn't care less. I told him what I thought, and he was contrite, but pointed out that he had learned in Tibet never, *never* to lose your horse, for a person's life in that vast country depended on it. He had reacted instinctively to this when he went after my horse.

We walked back, but I had so enjoyed the ride before the fall that I said I would like to do it again sometime. A few days later George asked me if I would like to go on a Tibetan horse-riding picnic with him and some of his Tibetan friends, and I gladly accepted. Apparently this caused some speculation among Molly and my friends about 'something happening between these two'; but Muriel had dismissed this, saying, 'Meg is much too sensible to have anything to do with an adventurer like that.'

On the day of the picnic there were about twenty Tibetans, men and women, laughing and shouting as they pranced around on their excited Tibetan horses, while Tibetan servants loaded up other horses and mules with picnic paraphernalia. George was dressed in a loose, white Tibetan silk shirt, riding breeches and riding boots, and looked very much at home amongst them. I felt a bit nervous, as the Tibetan horse I had been given to ride was quite different from the placid farm horse, and I was having difficulty in controlling it as it caught the restless excitement of the occasion. George eased alongside me and with an encouraging smile said to keep close to him at all times.

We took off up the trail to a mountain village several miles away, and we never stopped galloping. It was mad, unbelievably mad. The Tibetan idea of a horse race, George had informed me, was not just to get to a distant spot first, but to test a rival's skill and nerve on the way there. On the narrow mountain trail twenty horses, with shouting and laughing riders, jockeyed to pass where there was scarcely room for two. The rider on the outside of the trail had his or her stirrups right over a five-thousand-foot drop to the raging river far below. They drove their horses, slithering and slipping, up the steep mountainside to get ahead of the rider in front, with nerveless abandon. I was in the centre of this mêlée somewhere, with George fighting to keep near me to control my almost frantic horse which was striving to pull ahead. This was seen as a provocation to the others, who interpreted it as a challenge to pass at any cost, and eventually I just decided to enjoy the suicidal experience and was carried away in exhilaration beyond any thoughts of safety.

It was a glorious, unforgettable day. The picnic spot was in an open glade in the forests, looking out over the serrated ranks of snow mountains disappearing into the hazy blue distance. The Tibetans were uproariously friendly, laughing at my expressions as I drank their rancid yak-butter tea and barley beer, teasing me with bawdy stories of George's supposed relations with women in the wholly different culture of Tibet. They sang and danced to gypsy-like but oriental melodies. The meal was a feast of meats broiled over open fires, and eaten by hand when cut with the sharp daggers taken from their girdles, together with a kind of porridge made from barley flour mixed with tea and called *tsamba*. There were soup noodles, and rice, and every kind of vegetable in a variety of fragrant sauces. I noted with amusement that George was a different person among his beloved Tibetans.

The picnic eventually drew to a close in late afternoon, and the Tibetans raced away homewards in a repeat of the earlier race. George and I dropped behind, content to let the horses pick their own pace down the trail while we talked. Then, as the sun set over the snow-covered mountain ranges in a blaze of reds and purples and scarlets and yellows, we got off our horses and walked ahead of them, leading them by the reins, our eyes drinking in the magnificent land and sky panorama unfolding before us. In the all-encompassing beauty and silence, broken only by the slipping of the horses' hooves on the rough stones of the trail, I acknowledged to myself that I was in love.

By the time we got home and had bathed and changed, the others had finished dinner and gone out. As Lungma, the McCabes' Nepalese cook, served us dinner we ate slowly, our conversation becoming more personal, with longer silences between. I could feel my appetite diminishing as the tension increased, and I suspected that it was because George was sensing, as I was, that we were approaching some commitment in our relationship that we had not reached before in our experience. We were no longer just making friendly conversation, but seeking responses from each other which would confirm what was happening in us and between us. Both of us seemed to be conscious that we were entering hitherto unexplored territory in our relationship, and that with each forward step into new yielded intimacies there was a corresponding admission of acceptance of each other with its responsibilities. I waited with a tremulous anticipation.

After one long silence George said hesitantly, 'Meg, I don't know how to say this, but I must say something for your sake as well as my own. I love you, but I can't marry you. I am committed to serving God in Tibet, and I expect to return there just as soon as I can, and there is no place for a wife in my life that I can see.'

I felt a huge relief at his words. 'I love you, too,' I replied, happy for the present that he felt as I did. 'I understand your situation, for I am also committed to serving God in Ludhiana.'

I had only five days left of my holiday, and to the shock and consternation of the Kalimpong community, especially the missionaries, we spent the five days constantly in each other's company. Molly McCabe was overjoyed, but Muriel Clemenger was dismayed. We were deeply, passionately, in love, and didn't care who knew it, taking all that the present offered.

When I returned to Ludhiana we wrote to each other every few days, long letters, discussing hopes and fears, beliefs and values, work and play, pleasures and disappointments—and longings, longings, longings. Both of our lives had been turned upside down by the tempestuous love that engulfed us, but in our individual vocations there seemed to be no bridge that could bring us together. What had George's adventurous, itinerant life in vast and remote spaces in Central Asia in common with my own structured academic and medical existence within the four walls of lecture room and operating theatre? What had George's raging intellectual and spiritual hunger for God in common with my own calm acceptance of divine immanence?

One incident of that time stood out above all others. Until I had met George my Christian experience had been fairly orthodox and uneventful, except for the excitements associated with my work as a surgeon. But my visit to the Tibetan border, and the completely new world that I had been introduced to through his experiences, had brought a new dimension into my spiritual life. This was especially true in the realm of demonism, which I had first encountered in my early conversations with George regarding his investigations of Tibetan demonism with Prince Peter of Greece and Denmark.

Shortly after I returned to Ludhiana from Kalimpong, I was lying awake one night thinking over our situation when I became conscious of an overwhelming 'presence of evil' in my room. I was totally disorientated for I had never experienced anything like it in all my life. In my sheltered upbringing I had scarcely known fear, and this threatening, suffocating terror paralysed me. I don't know how long I lay there, unable to move or think, but slowly I began to remember some of the things George had told me about how he combated the evil attacks on him and Geoff Bull in Tibet through prayer and Scriptures.

I gradually took control of my thoughts and then commanded the 'evil presence' filling the room to depart in the Name of the Lord Jesus Christ. Miraculously it worked, and I was freed. But for a long time afterwards I was aware of 'its' threatening presence on the edge of my consciousness as I went about my daily work.

I discussed it in my letters to George, and we concluded that it was Satan's attempt to frighten me away from an association with George in the kind of ruthless spiritual conflict in which he was engaged in Tibet. Also, a personal demonstration to me by God of the kind of spiritual powers that were able to overcome such diabolical terrors when His servants were confronted by them.

Letters were of no use in providing all the answers I sought in my spiritually and emotionally disrupted life. I had to see George once more. We had parted in June, 1952, never expecting to meet again, and it was now September. I had two weeks' leave due me from the previous summer, and so I decided to return to Kalimpong, come what may, in search of a final answer.

When we met, the decision, unplanned, was already made. We did not care what the future held for either of us, so long as we faced it together. We both believed that God had brought us together, so it was up to God to sort out the problems which seemed so insoluble to us.

My contract with the Ludhiana Medical College was due to expire in the autumn of 1953, and George's book about his epic journey across unexplored Tibet, *Tibetan Journey*, was expected to be published about the same time, so we decided to get married in Scotland in September, 1953.

George left for home in June, a few months before me, with an unenviable task facing him. Neither of our families were very pleased with the thought of our getting married, for reasons of their own. Unthinkingly, I had made it even more difficult for George, for I had written home saying that I 'had to get married in September', meaning that I wanted to be married at the start of my leave, for we had planned to return to Kalimpong. I did not explain this, and I gave the impression that I had to get married because I was pregnant!

Fortunately, George's sense of humour was able to cope with the consequences of this. His brother, Bill, had also increased my family's fears by declaring cheerfully, 'Meg won't have her troubles to seek if she marries George.' To make matters worse, Bill had gone to visit my family dressed in his kilt, and my father believed—as did many Scots Brethren—that this was 'women's clothing' denounced and forbidden in the Old Testament.

When George finally visited Aberdeen my father, for domestic reasons, was unable to put him up in his home, and George stayed with the Presbyterian minister whom I wanted to marry us, Willie Still, a friend of mine from university days. But my father had invited him to have supper with him, and George went there soon after his arrival in Aberdeen.

My father opened the door and, after inviting George to enter, asked him how he was keeping. As he took his coat he asked George how I was keeping. Then, as he escorted him into the sitting-room, and they were seated, he said to George, 'Tell me, Mr Patterson, what do you think is the difference in significance between the Tabernacle and the Temple?' To a Brethren father it was more important to establish the ability of his proposed son-in-law to interpret the Scriptures, than to know his future prospects or intentions.

George, of course, had been brought up in this environment and knew what was required, but with his whimsical sense of humour, he now said to my father: 'Mr Ingram, I could answer this in the way that you hope and is generally accepted, or I could answer it in a way that is permissible but debatable among Brethren, or I could tell you what I really think. Since I am hoping to have a long and profitable relationship with you, I am going to tell you what I think about this, and all other subjects you may raise.

You may not approve, but it will keep us both interested.'
After I got home I gathered that was the beginning of a
series of lengthy, and often impassioned, debates between
them about the Scriptures. My father was a rigid
traditionalist, but he did know his Bible, and he was not
prepared to give up strong convictions without a fight.

But he met his match in George. George was always
polite—but inflexible. His knowledge of the Bible was
greater than my father's, and he had read more and
experienced more in his travels. So when my father
expressed his objections to my stated intention of being
married in an interdenominational church by a Presbyterian
minister, and that he wanted me to be married in a Brethren
Gospel Hall by a Brethren evangelist, he expected George's
approval and co-operation. He was struck speechless when
George told him, 'I don't mind if she is married in a Tibetan
monastery by a Tibetan monk. The Scriptures teach that a
marriage is made in heaven, and that the civil ceremony is
only a social observance.'

That was bad enough, but it was nothing compared with
George's further declaration that, since our marriage was
already made in heaven, when he was asked by the
officiating minister, 'Do you take this woman to be your
lawfully wedded wife?' he said he felt it was only Scripturally
appropriate that he should reply 'I have' and not 'I do'!
Everyone, even the minister, was in a panic about this—with
all its embarrassing implications—until the moment during
the ceremony was reached and George answered 'I do',
according to custom. His wayward sense of humour took
some getting used to, I found.

The wedding took place on 12 September, 1953, in the
magnificent chapel of King's College, Aberdeen University.
My bridesmaid was from my first group of graduate students
(who had been so 'terrified' of me!). She had come to
Britain to study for a higher degree in surgery. She was
dressed in a brilliant orange Indian sari of clinging geor-
gette, which caught the attention of all the photographers.

The ceremony was attended by many leading figures from among the Brethren. G. H. Lang, a noted Bible scholar and longtime friend of George's, made his last public appearance to give a short but memorable address on Jesus' attendance at the wedding in Cana of Galilee. Ironically, because the media turned out in force, and the wedding was reported, with photographs, in the Sunday newspapers the following day, many Brethren assemblies cancelled George's later engagements to address their gatherings—as if it were his responsibility. The sequence of events before, during and after our marriage was afterwards embellished in hundreds of conversations across the country to add to George's burgeoning reputation, and to my great amusement I found myself the object of a considerable amount of sympathy for the 'predicament' of being married to him.

If what was known was controversial, or hilarious, depending on one's point of view, what was not known was even more disputatious and hysterical. We had used up what little money we had in the preparations for the wedding, and I even had to scratch around for the money to help George pay for the marriage licence.

Then, we had arranged for a short honeymoon at a small hotel in Banchory, beside the River Dee near Aberdeen. But a few days after we got there George suddenly announced that we were flying to the Shetlands, off the north coast of Scotland, to spend several days with relatives of mine. When I asked him how we could afford to do that he just smiled provocatively.

We had a wonderful time there, and then left for Edinburgh en route for England where we had arranged to spend a few days with my brother Ed, who was working in a hospital in Leeds.

While we were in Edinburgh, walking down the famed Princes Street, with its spectacular castle and gardens on one side and shops on the other, we stopped outside a famous fashion shop. I had never been very interested in clothes, partly because I had never had the money to spend on them, and partly because I had been too busy studying and working to find time to buy them. In India, with the small salary I had, I had been glad to find old charity cast-off clothing sent to missionaries which fitted me. So, it was with only casual female interest, coupled with honeymoon euphoria, that I was gazing at the *haute couture* dresses in the window, when George suddenly surprised me by opening the door and walking inside the shop.

It seemed vast, with a few gilt chairs scattered on the dove-grey carpet, with gold and lilac walls and huge crystal chandeliers. I looked at George, and he gave the tantalising, mocking smile he had smiled the night I had first met him (he had since told me that he had acted as obnoxiously as he did because Molly had said she was determined to get him 'respectably' matched with one of us, and he wanted to put us off!), which I was beginning to recognise as a prelude to some reckless action on his part that no one approved.

An elegantly gowned and coiffed saleswoman approached us with raised eyebrows and a supercilious half-smile. 'May I help you?' she asked, her eyes checking our appearance. I looked at George, wondering what he was up to.

His smile deepened, and he answered, 'Yes, please. My wife would like to see some of your dresses or suits.'

I could only gaze at him in shocked surprise. I had no interest in buying a dress; I knew we had no money; and even if we had I wouldn't be buying in a place like this.

The woman saw my expression, and her superciliousness edged closer to contempt. 'What would madam like to see? Any colour preference? Or couturier? Or type?'

George saved me by interrupting blandly. 'Perhaps you could just show us something for a start? What size, dear?' he asked, turning to me.

'Eight,' I stammered, trying to give him a warning look without alerting the lynx-eyed saleswoman. He was impervious, ignoring me and smiling dismissal to the saleswoman.

As she walked away across the grey-carpeted expanse to the glass-fronted cabinets along the walls I whispered wildly to George, 'What are you doing? I can't try on dresses here.'

'Why not?' he asked with maddening pretended innocence and surprise. 'It's a very nice place in which to try on dresses.' And he walked over to sit down on one of the gilt chairs. I could only follow and do likewise.

The saleswoman returned with a dress over her arm, her smile gone and her voice brisk, cold and dismissive. Obviously, she had decided we were not the sort of clientèle her establishment wanted, and she was taking action accordingly. I felt relieved, not offended.

'This is the only dress we have in madam's size,' she said in a clipped, West Edinburgh accent, 'and it costs eighty-five pounds.'

George looked from her to the dress, and back again. 'Do you like it?' he asked me. I shook my head negatively, hoping that this meant the end of the charade.

'Will you fetch the manager, or your superior?' George said coldly—I couldn't believe I was hearing aright—'I didn't come in here to be told by you that you have only one dress in one size, or to be told the price before I asked. So will you find someone who will give me what I do want?'

The woman didn't know what to do, or where to look. Neither did I. This was a George I hadn't seen—cold, ruthless, dominating—but to what purpose? I thought numbly. The saleswoman turned away abruptly, and George gave me a pleasant smile. She returned a few moments later with a suave, well-dressed gentleman.

George spoke to him. 'I would like something for my wife. Size eight. And do you have a model to display it for us?' he asked confidently.

'Certainly, sir,' the manager replied courteously. 'Come this way.' He walked towards an arched salon, with two gilt chairs, on the far side. 'If you and madam will sit here I will arrange for a model to display some clothes. Have you any preferences?'

George looked at me, but again I could only shake my head. 'Just bring a few different styles and colours,' he suggested, 'and, if it isn't too much trouble, I would like to see on a model the blue suit you have displayed in the window.'

'No trouble at all, sir,' the manager assured him, and left.

George smiled happily at me. 'Enjoying yourself?' he asked mischievously. 'If you see anything you like, try it on. It doesn't cost anything to do that. They're used to it. The rich do it all the time. I'll handle the rest.'

For the next hour or so a model paraded in front of us with a variety of dresses and costumes, including the one we had been looking at when George started this whole episode. I had mentioned then that I liked it, and I repeated this again when I saw it on the model. It was a dress of a stunning shade of blue in simple but classic cut, with a beehive-shaped, blocked semi-cape of the same colour.

'Try it on, dear,' George suggested remorselessly, when I said I preferred this outfit above the others.

'What are we–' I began to ask, and stopped as George just smiled.

It fitted me perfectly, and transformed me completely. I hardly recognised myself as the same person when I gazed at my stylish reflection in the several mirrors. George's approving nod to me as I entered the salon confirmed this, and the manager agreed.

'Do you have a hat and pair of shoes that will match this outfit, or could you send out for them?' George asked the now-enthusiastic manager, and he nodded happily and hurried away to comply.

When he had left the salon George said to me, 'I wanted this to be a complete surprise wedding present from me to you. I had news from the publishers that the orders and sales for my book were so good that they were sending a large cheque, and asking how I wished it to be paid. I told them to pay it straight into my bank account. I wanted to get something for you that would epitomise the beauty and joy and daring of our relationship. This is my gift to you, from the first proceeds of my first book about my first journey across unexplored Tibet. Enjoy it.'

The hat and shoes were a perfect match, and we were shown to the door by the complimentary manager. I felt the happiest—and best-dressed—woman in the world. The incongruity of an expensive *haute couture* outfit when we had no other money, or jobs, and we were returning without financial support to the mountains of one of the remotest areas in the world, just heightened the intoxication. After all, it was no more incongruous than the apparent irreconcilability of the two different sets of skills and commitments God had given to us. I wore that outfit many times in many places over the next twenty years, and nothing else I ever wore gave me the sheer pleasure it did.

The honeymoon over, George was booked to speak at meetings and conferences across the country. He was one of the few Europeans to have lived inside Tibet, he was one of the even fewer missionaries to have reached there, he was the first person ever to have made the journey from China to India described in *Tibetan Journey*, and he was in great demand.

But he had been very disillusioned when he was in China and India by the post-war colonialist and paternalist missionary practices; he was opposed to oppressive and exploitative political systems in Asia; he was apprehensive about the threat posed by the new Chinese Communist régime; and he was excited by the emergence and potential of the national indigenous Christian leaders of China and India and other countries of Asia.

His passionate addresses about these issues, with their implication that many widely respected missionaries were guilty of Scripturally unacceptable practices and that leading Brethren in Britain were conniving in them, infuriated the old-school, stereotyped elders of the Brethren assemblies, while they fired the vision of the younger members who had suspected that there was something wrong because of the widespread impotence of Brethren witness. But George was a revolutionary as well as a visionary. It was not enough just to get people talking about circumstances; he wanted action taken to correct abuses. He wanted traditional elders removed from office, and replaced with spiritually gifted men. He wanted the sterile traditionalist practices which had brought Brethren into disrepute changed, and new relevant practices based on Scriptural principles introduced. He warned that the writing was on the wall for Brethren churches if radical changes were not made.

At the Annual Missionary Meetings of the Brethren, held in Westminster, London, before two to three thousand members from all over the country, George was taken aside by one of the leading Brethren and warned 'not to cause trouble'. When he asked what he was supposed to speak about, he was told to give some interesting episodes from his travels in Tibet. Ironically, at the same meeting Professor Bruce was also one of the scheduled speakers and he gave an address about how the early Church was not an organisation, and Paul's missionary work was mobile and not fixed. This was no more than George had been preaching, but as Fred Bruce said, 'George represented a radical viewpoint.'

In my earlier conversations with George, and in our later correspondence, we had discussed many of these issues. To someone like myself who had been brought up in the Brethren traditionalist setting, and where rebellion against it meant moving out of Brethren into one of the denominations, it had come as a shock to hear George's radical understanding of the Scriptures. To him, God, not Marx, was the first true revolutionary; God was the initiator of total change, in individuals and nations, especially in circumstances of spiritual decline and impotence. His own early period of rebellion in Scotland against the all-encompassing status quo sterility had convinced him, theoretically and from the Scriptures, that the fault must lie with men and women and not with God. Then, his exposure to the dynamism of Christianity in indigenous Christian churches in China, and later in India when he arrived there, had confirmed his Scriptural convictions. He had seen the Scriptural past, and it worked; and he had seen the Scriptural present, and it worked; and he was determined to see a Scriptural future in Britain and the West, whatever it cost.

It was an exciting vision for the younger element, but it terrified the older traditionalists and they clubbed together to put a stop to his preaching in Brethren assemblies—but without observing Scriptural principles of spiritual discipline. One of the leading men in Brethren circles, when challenged by George about this breach of Biblical teaching, said: 'But, George, we are afraid to meet with you to discuss these matters, as you might put it into a book'! George's dry reply was, 'I thought you believed all that we are doing is being recorded in a book by God, anyway.'

There was nothing left to do in Britain, and George had decided to write a book about his spiritual experiences, tentatively entitled *God's Fool*, which could be done in Kalimpong. I had decided to go where he was, and to let God deal with the problem of using my surgical skills. I was now part of George's vision, I believed. It was God who had sent me to India. It was God who had led me to Kalimpong. It was God who had brought us together. Our individually different lives were inextricably bound up with the still-unknown purposes of God. I couldn't see how I could change the world, but I certainly wanted to be there with George when it happened. My family and friends were very unhappy about this; but, then, George's family were also very unhappy about what marriage to me would mean for him and his vision. Fortunately, we were very happy with each other.

- 3 -

My Own Hospital in Darjeeling

When we returned to Kalimpong in 1954 we stayed with George and Molly McCabe until we found a suitable place of our own. Since we were living on the Dr Graham's Homes' compound I was asked to be their Medical Officer, which I agreed to do. It was a job which an elderly retired doctor had been doing before me, and professionally I found it tedious in the extreme. I had become so accustomed since I graduated to dealing with complex, challenging, life-and-death surgical situations, that it was difficult to adjust to treating mundane aches and pains.

The only local hospital was a Church of Scotland mission hospital whose Superintendent, Dr Craig, was a physician and not a surgeon. It had an even more rudimentary operating theatre than Ludhiana Medical College had when I first went there, and there was no one who could give an adequate anaesthetic. There wasn't even a cylinder of oxygen. So it was only possible for me to do a limited amount of surgery, mostly emergencies from the local community. Meanwhile I attended to the ailments of the school children, the missionaries and some of the townspeople.

We found a lovely bungalow to rent about a mile outside Kalimpong, with an unobstructed view of the whole Kanchenjunga mountain range. From there George once again became deeply involved in the complex, secretive and dangerous international politics being conducted in this sensitive Himalayan region.

In our intense conversations during the limited time we spent together when we first met, I had learned something of the exciting circumstances in which he was involved. He had left his English missionary companion, Geoff Bull, and his Khamba Tibetan friends in East Tibet at the latters' request, in order to travel as quickly as possible to India across unexplored Tibet to seek help from the Indian, British, American governments, or the United Nations Organisation, to resist the threatening Chinese Communist army on Tibet's eastern frontier.

Considering his obscure background, he had been remarkably successful in reaching influential officials and diplomats with his news and pleas, but he was not successful in persuading them to help. When he had attempted to return to Tibet within the six months he had agreed with his Khamba friends in East Tibet, he had been hindered by the sudden onset of the monsoon rains sweeping away roads and bridges; then a major catastrophic earthquake, with its epicentre from his point of departure in India to his point of arrival in Tibet; and, finally, by a sudden attack of deep thrombophlebitis in both legs which hospitalised him for several months. During this extended period of enforced reflection he was convinced that God wanted him to remain in Kalimpong for a purpose yet unknown.

While he was in hospital in Kalimpong the Chinese Communists had attacked in East Tibet, as he had warned the outside world, and begun their military occupation of Tibet. Thousands of Tibetans of all classes fled to India, most of them to Kalimpong. The wealthy Tibetans bought large houses, and the others found whatever places they could. This exodus, in turn, brought thousands of visitors to Kalimpong—media representatives, intelligence-gathering spies, scholars, government officials, and tourists—and Kalimpong became to the Himalayan region what Lisbon was to Western Europe during the Second World War, a hive of clandestine activities and rumours.

George had mentioned something of this in our many

conversations, but these had not prepared me for the reality of the cloak-and-dagger circumstances in which we began our married life. With his knowledge of the Tibetan language George had been deeply involved in all sorts of lawful and unlawful activities before leaving for Scotland and our wedding. His own contacts inside Tibet, especially those in East Tibet where the fierce Khamba tribesmen were resisting the occupying Chinese armies, meant that he was in constant demand both as a source of information and as a language interpreter. Some of these situations were innocuous, but many of them required great secrecy and caution, depending on who wanted what hidden from others.

The news that George was receiving from his Khamba friends in East Tibet was that they were preparing for major revolt against the Chinese occupation forces, and not just nuisance insurrections. When he reported this serious development to the *Guardian*, the editor chose to repress the article, and printed instead the official Indian pro-Chinese accounts that all was peaceful inside Tibet. Two journalist friends of George's, Guy Wint and Roderick MacFarquahar, persuaded him to continue writing for the *Daily Telegraph* instead, and the editor assured him that they would carry all factual reports. His articles drew attention from the nastier elements within the various interested governments, and his friends in the Indian security informed him that they had information that the Communists in the area were out to kill him and offered to provide him with a firearms permit. He thanked them but refused, confusing them with his wry quote, 'I am immortal till my work is done.'

Such casual disregard did not impress George's Tibetan servant, Loshay. Loshay had been provided as a personal servant to George by the East Tibetan chieftain, Pangdatshang, with whom George had lived during his sojourn in Tibet. The feudal custom was that such a servant was more like a 'blood-brother', responsible for his master's personal safety as well as his possessions. Loshay had taken his responsibilities seriously, and there were many stories of how he had saved George's life on occasions.

Loshay had taken it on himself to provide an unseen escort service for George when he went out, especially when he was returning late at night. He was infuriated to discover that there were often as many as three people following George, and it was difficult to tell whether they were police, security or political assassins; this meant that he was hindered from taking the direct action he was accustomed to using, for George had warned him that in India he would be arrested and imprisoned for harming or killing people as he had done in Tibet. Loshay had had a formidable reputation in Tibet as a fighter with hands or swords.

George had told me an amusing episode that had occurred soon after we had met, when George had told Loshay about me. He had been explaining to Loshay, without success, what 'engagement' or 'betrothal' meant in Western Christian terms. That night George had been wakened by a sound which, after lying tensely silent, he identified as coming from inside the room where he was sleeping. He had edged himself within reach of the bedside table, then, suddenly, switched on the light and hurled the lamp at where he had heard the sound, jumping out of bed at the same time. It was Loshay who was standing there, blinking.

'What do you think you're doing?' George demanded, when he had got over his surprise.

'Where is she?' asked Loshay, looking from George to the bed. 'I wanted to see you in bed with your woman.'

It had been a cause of great merriment to the Tibetans, especially Loshay as George's 'arranger of affairs', that he had politely refused the Tibetan practice of accepting women when they travelled, on the basis of it being against his religion. When this had happened in Tibet Loshay had enquired, with a grin, whether George wanted boys instead, as that was the accepted requirement for Tibetan monks. It was against this background of George's celibacy that he had decided to see for himself the custom of Westerners by slipping into George's bedroom unannounced.

I had become accustomed to being seen by Loshay at unexpected times, and in various stages of undress, as Tibetans were very relaxed about such things as knocking on doors, and also Loshay was constantly on the watch for unwanted intruders at all times of the night. But it tended to be acutely embarrassing for our visitors.

On one occasion we had three young women missionaries staying with us. During the night we heard a scream, and George threw himself out of bed and was on his way to help when I had to shout at him that he had no clothes on. He grabbed something, and we went through to the guest rooms.

We found the window open, and the young women in a state of panic. One of them had awakened and found a man in the room, and had screamed. The man jumped out of the window, and by the time George and Loshay got there he had disappeared into the darkness outside. It was only after the excitement had died down, and we were having a cup of tea together, that it dawned on everybody the young women were still in their nightdresses—and they were see-through! It bothered them more than it bothered Loshay. The Tibetans were not voyeuristic as they had a natural attitude towards sexual matters.

If our family and friends in the West were confused and bewildered about our decisions and activities, this was even more true of our friends and acquaintances in Kalimpong and India. On the one hand, we were seen to be leading a very high-profile social life, with colourful, media-reported adventures in the exciting underworld of Himalayan politics; while, on the other hand, George was known both locally and nationally as a Bible teacher.

He told me that when he first arrived in Kalimpong, he had met the remarkable Indian evangelist Bakht Singh, who was on a preaching visit there. Bakht Singh had heard

George preach and had asked him to join him in his preaching tours. Since then, George had often taken part in these evangelistic campaigns in different parts of India with the indigenous Indian churches. With Bakht Singh and a few other Indian preachers they would go into villages, towns and cities and, starting with only a few people and a little money, build up huge audiences numbering thousands, with hundreds of converts, establish new churches and supporting teaching programmes, and then move on.

This was the kind of activity George loved, and he was torn between his desire to commit himself to this, and the commitment to following and learning of God in the miasmic jungle of politics. It was not that he had to choose one or the other, for he was preaching far more and to many more people than the majority of 'orthodox' missionaries, at the same time as he was busily engaged in the complex and dangerous world of Asian politics and espionage. It was just that it would have simplified his life, and eliminated much misunderstanding; but it would not have provided the framework within which he was following a fascinating path into the revelation of God to him in a twentieth-century context. And it was in this vision that I could join with him, and support him—much more than the political circumstances, which only interested me peripherally— because I, too, was learning profound lessons about the ways of God I had never known.

So, in Kalimpong, one of the great mysteries in social circles in that 'nest of spies' was: who, really, was George working for? The Russians said, 'British government.' The Chinese said, 'CIA.' And the missionaries said, 'The Devil.'

While all this was going on I had to make a sudden return to Ludhiana for the removal of an ovarian cyst which had begun to trouble me. We decided to travel from Calcutta by car when some business friends offered to sell us a Riley Sports convertible, and a missionary friend whom George had known on the Chinese border of Tibet, Vik Hjelmervik, agreed to travel with us. Vik was a highly skilled engineer, and it set our minds at rest having him with us.

There was little room for luggage in the small sports car when the three of us were squeezed in, but we travelled up the Grand Trunk Road from Calcutta to New Delhi, and on to Ludhiana, over three days' journey, without any trouble.

The operation was completed without complications, but I was dismayed to learn that it could interfere with our hopes of having children. I was thirty-three years of age and George was two years older. After a week or so we began our return journey, with a side trip to Agra to see the magnificent Taj Mahal—built by the Moghul ruler, Shah Jehan, as a memorial to his beloved wife—by sunrise and moonlight.

We tried to do most of our driving in early morning or in the cool of the evening, resting during the blinding heat of the day, taking turns at driving. We had just left Agra and New Delhi behind us soon after dawn, and George was driving while Vik and I dozed, when the car gave a sudden lurch and there were loud shouts. George righted the swerving car, then accelerated away quickly. It appeared that George was driving at a steady sixty miles an hour down the middle of the tarmac road, with his eyes on an approaching line of loaded donkeys being driven to market by some peasants. He was passing them, uneventfully, when there was a jerk, and the car swerved to the side, and there were the shouts. George thought that one of the donkeys must have stepped into the road as the car passed, and the ropes tying on the load must have caught the V-arm of the canvas hood and tilted the donkey over. When he saw that everything was all right, and nobody was hurt, including the donkey, he had quickly driven away to avoid extortionate demands for compensation.

We had scarcely settled down after this episode, and the car was rolling along smoothly in the pleasant morning heat, when there was a jolt and George was struggling to keep the car on the road. Beside him I saw, with horror, a wheel bouncing high in the air and then careering away in a series of higher bounces across the fields. I could not believe my eyes when George, having successfully fought the car to a standstill, grabbed the camera from the glove compartment and, with shaking hands, began taking photographs of the disappearing wheel. It was the last amusing happening for some time.

When Vik had assessed the damage he found that the wheel-locking mechanism was stripped, and we were about a hundred miles from a large city likely to have any replacement for a Riley Sports model. Vik took off in a passing donkey-and-trap contraption to reach the nearest bus or train for Benares, while we rigged up a mosquito net over the convertible and settled down at the side of the road to await his return. After a restless night spent in the car, we woke to find ourselves being stared at by silent, curious peasants. Fortunately, Vik arrived late the next day, and after repairing the wheel we resumed our journey.

We had only driven for a few hours when there was a suspicious rattle, and Vik sat forward to listen. When it happened again, he shook his head and started to say 'Stop' when there was a clatter from the engine. I think Vik said we had 'stripped a big end' or something. Anyway, it meant we were now again marooned at the side of the endless road between New Delhi and Calcutta, with another side-trip for Vik—this time to Calcutta, to get the damaged cylinders re-lined and bring them back to be refitted to the car.

It took him several days to get this done, and meanwhile George and I found a nearby 'dak bungalow', or government cottage for travelling officials, where we could sleep and get basic Indian food, while keeping an eye on the car. When Vik did eventually turn up he did it in style. He brought with him some of our Calcutta friends, and a huge hamper of food and drinks. When they had gone I settled down to watch while Vik and George tediously, hour after hour, scraped away at the newly lined cylinder with knives to get it to fit. When it finally did, the fit was so tight that the engine would not turn over, so we had to wait for hours until we could get a passing motorist to give us a tow to get started. Once started, we decided that, come what may, we were not going to stop again until we arrived in Calcutta—even if it meant driving all night.

We had left Loshay with our friends in Calcutta, and so we now had four people in the small Riley sports car for the four-hundred-mile drive to Kalimpong. We were not really surprised when it broke down again halfway there. This time we were in a fairly large town, and we had it towed into a repair shop. But there was no public transport available so we thumbed a lift, George and I together, and Loshay and Vik together, in two separate trucks travelling to Siliguri, the railhead in north Bengal serving the foothills of the Himalayas.

There was no room in the driver's cabin, as there were two others in beside the driver, and we had to sit on the top of the loaded boxes high above the cab and hold on by the binding ropes as the truck bumped and roared its way northwards. We were still some way from Siliguri, and it was getting dark, when we approached a roadblock and officials of some sort. Instead of slowing down, to our consternation the driver suddenly swung the truck off the road and accelerated away across the fields, jolting and swerving madly. The sudden manoeuvre must have taken the officials by surprise for when, after stopping and cutting his engine, there were no signs of pursuit in the enveloping darkness, the driver shouted for George and me to get down and walk. From what they were saying we gathered that they must have been carrying contraband of some kind and they were going to go around the roadblock somewhere. They did not want us with them. After finding our way back to the road, we got another lift into Siliguri, and, as we had planned, we met up with Vik and Loshay at the railway restaurant. This ended my trip to Ludhiana for my first surgical operation, and convalescence.

Shortly afterwards, however, I nearly lost Vik in an operation. I had to do a simple corrective operation on Vik for troublesome haemorrhoids, and I arranged to do the operation in the Church of Scotland hospital in Kalimpong. A new young doctor had arrived from Scotland who had aspirations to be a surgeon, but who had had no experience. Unfortunately, he was opinionated and reckless, and he had already lost several patients because of his ignorance and carelessness. While I would not use him as an assistant at the operating table, I had to use him as an anaesthetist.

Anaesthetic procedures were primitive and a fine balance had to be maintained with the ether-drip technique and my surgical activities on the patient. Once I had Vik anaesthetised I concentrated on him at the bottom end of the table. Suddenly, at a critical point in the operation, I was aware that Vik had stopped breathing and, when I looked at him, his face was blue! The young doctor was so busy watching me that he had overdosed Vik. I had to stop everything and apply emergency measures (the hospital had no oxygen) to save his life. It was almost ten minutes before he started breathing spontaneously, and I could scrub up again to complete the operation.

Within a year I had to have another operation, in even more dangerous circumstances. I had gone to the Homes for my daily medical rounds, and in the afternoon I felt a sharp pain in my abdomen that grew steadily worse. I had to lie down, and I asked the Homes' matron to send for the town doctor, Dr Rao, and for George. I suspected, from the intensity of the sudden pain, that I had developed some sort of bowel strangulation, a condition that I could easily deal with in others—if I had an operating theatre—but I seriously doubted whether there was anybody within hundreds of miles of Kalimpong who could help me.

Dr Rao wanted to put me on morphine to ease the pain, but I asked him to hold off until George could find a surgeon. I knew it was going to be a critical operation, and I didn't want to be so dulled with morphine that the surgeon might be hindered in making a diagnosis. But when George tried to find the surgeon from the government hospital in

Darjeeling, some forty miles away, he was out of town. George then tried to fly a surgeon up from Calcutta but was told that all planes were grounded as a bad monsoon storm was expected.

On the fourth day of the attack my condition deteriorated rapidly, and George had me moved to the local Church of Scotland hospital, with the help of Prince Peter of Greece and Denmark, who had the only vehicle in Kalimpong that could take a stretcher and negotiate the twisting roads to the hospital. By this time I had to take morphine for the excruciating pain and knew very little of what was happening. Later, I learned from George that his frantic efforts eventually produced *ten* doctors, but only one surgeon—the government surgeon from Darjeeling, whose main skills were eye surgery, and who arrived at midnight. Fortunately, the surgeon brought with him the necessary medical and surgical apparatus for emergencies.

After a lengthy conference of all ten doctors they called George in and told him they had a divided opinion about the possible cause of my condition; but that Dr Bromley, of the Tea Planters' Hospital in Darjeeling, a gynaecologist, who had been the first to see me after Dr Rao, and without morphine, had advised operating immediately. George said to operate, and three hours later he was told by the government surgeon that if he had not operated when he did I would have been dead by morning. Several feet of bowel were found to be gangrenous because of a closed-loop intestinal obstruction. The result of this was that after the operation I developed severe 'paralytic ileus' (paralysis of all bowel function), and, in addition to intense vomiting, my abdomen was distending to the size of an advanced pregnancy.

I was critically ill for several weeks, near death on a few occasions. At one point my pulse rate rose to an unbelievable 200 a minute, incompatible with survival, and George was called in to take my last messages to him and to my family. I learned later that the whole Kalimpong religious community—Buddhist, Hindu and Muslim, as well as Christian—were praying for me throughout this critical period. As I hovered on the brink of death, I still felt it was important to tell George that he was not to let anything stop him from returning to Tibet, or working for Tibet as he was doing. At once, although I was struggling on the edge of unconsciousness, I had the strangest conviction, considering the circumstances, that I was not going to die.

Afterwards, George told me that he had not accepted my impending death, and had made special prayer for my recovery at this low point. He also told me how my life was saved with whisky! Apparently, when the doctor left my room he went into the corridor where George was standing talking with Prince Peter and his wife, Princess Irene, who had come to see if there was anything they could do to help. Dr Craig told George about my critical condition, and that he had tried everything to get my paralysed bowel moving, without success. He said, finally, that there was only one thing left, but he could do nothing about it—give me whisky! Like George and me he was from Scotland (but a strict Presbyterian teetotaller), and he said that it was an old Scots remedy for paralysis of the bowel to give some drops of whisky in hot water every two hours. But unfortunately, he said to George, there was no Scotch whisky available in Kalimpong.

George turned to Prince Peter and Princess Irene and asked them if they had any whisky. They said they had and sent their driver to fetch it. He brought back a bottle of the best Scotch malt whisky, I was put on a regime of Dr Craig's remedy—and the critical peristalsis began, and my life was saved.

When I was at my lowest, I had an experience which I hesitate to describe as what is known as an 'out-of-the-body' experience. I felt I was walking towards a very bright glow, and I experienced intense joy. As my condition improved I felt reluctant to return to the reality waiting for me.

I recovered slowly, and because my operation had been

an emergency it was considered advisable that I should return to Britain for a check-up by specialists.

I was examined by my former chief, Norman Tanner, and pronounced reasonably clear of danger, but that I would have to watch out for any signs of recurrence of lesions. Also, there would be even more complications regarding having children.

I spent the major part of my convalescence with George's brother Bill and his wife Julia, who had a large farm of several thousand acres near Oban in Argyll, in the West Highlands. The farm was beautifully situated at the end of a remote glen, and the processional Standing Stones leading to the ancient palace of the Scottish kings of Dalriada were located on his lands.

When I was feeling well again it was decided that Bill and Julia should take advantage of our being available and take a long-postponed holiday, leaving their firstborn baby, Nicholas, with us. They had an excellent housemaid, the farm was well-equipped with all modern conveniences, including its own generator, so that, although we had no experience of running a farm, it was not a problem. The maid was from the local farming community, and Bill had cattlemen and shepherds to look after the livestock.

Bill and Julia had just left when the maid developed a bad attack of influenza, and I had to send her home. There seemed to be no problem with this unexpected development, as everything from the vacuum cleaner through the butter churner to the cow-milking process was done with the electricity from the generator. Unfortunately, the maid had only just gone when the generator broke down, and George was unable to repair it—or find anyone who could! We were still not greatly perturbed, although for me, it meant hand-washing clothes—including the baby's nappies—and we found candles for light, cooked on the large and efficient Aga stove, and said that the farm staff would sort out the problems next day.

In the morning, George heard unusual lowing from the

cattle and, when he went outside, he was suddenly reminded that the milking cows had been left out all night, and had not been milked the previous evening. That was part of the maid's tasks, and with her gone we had completely forgotten. George brought them into the byre, and began attempting to milk them by hand—something he had never done before!—because the automatic milking apparatus was useless with the generator broken. When I went outside to call him in for breakfast I found him struggling to get a cow's legs out of the milk bucket (three legs in the bucket, a record performance, Bill said later!), and only one teat out of four emptied.

Then George saw the dogs in the byre, and clasped his head. Another of the maid's tasks was to see that the dogs were shut up for the night. Bill had five dogs—two sheep-dogs, two gun dogs, and a dachshund—and, in addition, his mother's dog, a golden Labrador, was with him temporarily. They were all milling around quite happily.

As we went into the house we passed the henhouse. The door was open and some hens were in the yard, and some were in the trees—and inside there was bloody chaos. A fox or badger had got into the unlocked henhouse during the night and slaughtered about thirty hens and chickens. Another of the maid's tasks was to lock the henhouse—and we had overlooked this.

When we had finished a sombre breakfast, George returned to the byre to take up his milking job; at one teat every two hours he was going to take all day to milk the two cows—if his hands did not become paralysed before then! When I called him in for midmorning coffee, one of the shepherds—a taciturn individual, called Hugh, who rarely spoke—joined us as usual. After a few minutes he said, 'Were the dogs locked up last night?' We gave him a lugubrious explanation of our woes.

'There are seven sheep dead on the hill,' he said. When we just looked at him in stricken silence he added, 'They were all ready to lamb.'

When he went out to examine the dogs he found that the culprits had been the golden Labrador—its mouth was still bloody—and one of the collies. That meant they had to be put down before they did further damage.

A day or two later George noticed that one of Bill's riding horses, which had been on a high pasture, was in a nearby fenced field above the farmhouse. He went to see what had happened and found that Bill's thoroughbred had badly lacerated its chest and legs in jumping the fence, and the others had deep bleeding scratches on their legs from following. When George brought the horses back into the yard stables he had to cross a loosely built log-bridge over a deep stream; and the horse he was leading fell through the slipping logs.

That ended the saga of disasters in our first venture into farming. Bill and Julia took it with amazing calm and forgiveness, but they did not ask us, and we did not offer, to baby-sit for them again!

During my convalescence in Scotland I received a letter from Dr Bromley, who was one of the ten doctors summoned by George at the onset of my illness, and who was the Superintendent of the Tea Planters' Hospital in Darjeeling. He wanted to know if I would be interested in taking over his job as he was returning to England, and he would be happy to recommend me for the position.

Although he had not done much general surgery in the Tea Planters' Hospital, being a gynaecologist, he was certain that if I accepted the appointment the Board of Governors would co-operate in expanding the existing limited operating theatre facilities. It was a very exclusive hospital, serving only the tea planters' community in the famous Darjeeling and Dooars tea-growing districts of northern Bengal, with attached clinics in the many tea plantations in the area. The salary would be generous.

I was reluctant to take the post, mainly for two reasons: firstly, the thought of taking a large salary for my work in a poor country was distasteful after my experience in

Ludhiana; and, secondly, I disliked the thought of using my skills exclusively for a privileged class of people in that area. However, when George pointed out that Jesus healed the rich as well as the poor, and that the salary would not look so generous after paying India's crippling income taxes on foreigners, I agreed to accept the appointment. But I asked the Board of Governors for permission to use the hospital to treat the tea-garden labourers as well as the management personnel, and also the many needy missionaries and the sick of the surrounding Darjeeling community who could not afford to pay for treatment. At first they were reluctant because of the potentially huge costs which might be involved, but after a trial period in which I charged the wealthy an appropriate fee for my services—which was still much less than they would pay to travel to Calcutta for the same operations in expensive clinics—the Board saw that not only was I able to balance the accounts for the first time in the history of the hospital, but even had a surplus which could be used to buy better equipment.

The Tea Planters' Hospital, Darjeeling.
1959

Before I had the new equipment, however, I had to extemporise almost as much as I did at Ludhiana. I had no traction equipment, and so I co-opted Loshay to come into the operating theatre, dressed him in sterile gowns and used his great strength to separate broken bone ends which were overlapping so that I could align the bones to heal in a normal position.

I also used George, before I had sufficient skilled staff, to help with difficult cases. When a pregnant missionary wife was admitted for a Caesarean section, because of abnormal dilatation of the blood vessels of the uterus, I anticipated serious problems; the nearest blood bank was hundreds of miles away. I expected, when I incised the uterus, that there would be profuse bleeding, and so I required all the skilled nursing staff around the operating table for immediate assistance. It left us short of auxiliary help, and so George—who had had considerable medical experience in Tibet—was brought in to help out.

My worst fears were realised when the woman's uterus erupted with great gouts of blood, and there was high drama around the operating table while I got everything under control. I whipped the baby out and handed it to the matron, who quickly passed it to the staff nurse so that she could continue helping me with the sewing up. It was only when the excitement had died down, the operation was completed and the patient comfortable, that we discovered the baby had ended up with George—and he had had to apply the oxygen and do what was needful while everyone else was busy.

If George only had a minor part in my surgical activities he had a major role in introducing me to the benefits of homeopathy, which he had studied at the Missionary School of Medicine and the Royal Homeopathic Hospital in London and used extensively inside Tibet. I had the usual medical scepticism towards this form of treatment, and laughed when George recounted bizarre incidents when he had used it on animals as well as people.

However, a three-year-old child had been brought into the hospital one day with extensive burns, and was shrieking with pain. She had accidentally fallen into a tub of boiling water in a sitting position, and had been unable to get out for some time. She was raw flesh, from chest to knees, when she arrived. I was able to apply only the standard treatment of medicated tulle gras and painkillers. It did nothing to relieve her, and the hospital was filled with her screams.

George arrived at this point and asked what was wrong. I told him, and he said there was a dramatic homeopathic cure for burns. I said I was prepared to use it if he could find it. He went out into the bazaar and bought *urtica urens* (the common nettle plant) mother tincture, and a large jar of vaseline, and made a tub of the mixture. I applied it liberally, and within minutes the child had stopped her screams. She recovered completely within a remarkably short time.

I was now convinced, and asked George to teach me other remedies, and eventually I introduced a basic pack of homeopathic treatments into all the clinics.

Within a short time my operating theatre was the best equipped in north-east India. The 'Planters' Hospital', as it was known locally, quickly developed a reputation for successfully treating a variety of conditions, and the diversity of surgical cases I had to deal with from my experience in London, Ludhiana and Kalimpong was greater than I had ever known. In addition to the hospital, I expanded the tea-garden clinic activities until we had over two hundred of them, under the care of Indian doctors and nurses, feeding cases into the main hospital in Darjeeling. I was also made Medical Officer to five leading Catholic and Protestant colleges, as well as Honorary Medical Officer to the local Indian Army Ghurka Battalion and Medical Adviser to the Sherpa Mountaineering Association.

From being an underemployed school doctor, through my critical illness I had been precipitated into a promising medical and surgical situation greater than anything I could have dreamed of. I now had almost all that I had had in London, and then in Ludhiana, and much more, after apparently throwing it all away in marrying George. I had left my professional life in God's hands, for Him to solve the intractable problems, and He had given me more than I had desired.

This was a memorable period for me as each day I was presented with new administrative, medical and surgical challenges. As the flow of patients from Darjeeling and the surrounding districts increased I had to employ new medical and paramedical personnel, until I had a really impressive team.

This was confirmed when I was awakened early one morning with an emergency call. When I arrived at the hospital I found the staff in a state of crisis. Two famous journalists—Scott Leavitt and John Dominic, of *Time/Life*— had been driving up to one of the high ridges to photograph dawn over Kanchenjunga, and their jeep had gone over the side of the trail. Scott Leavitt was seriously injured, but John Dominic was only badly bruised. What was causing the trouble at the hospital was John Dominic's insistence that Scott Leavitt required the highest skilled surgery, and he was refusing to let my staff deal with his seriously injured colleague.

Even when I arrived he was insistent to the point of rudeness that there was no one who could adequately deal with his colleague in Darjeeling. Certainly, Scott Leavitt was in a bad way. The top of his skull had been laid open for about twelve inches front to back, and a deep gash in his forehead looked as if one eye were threatened. I knew the wounds had to be stitched immediately because of the ongoing loss of blood, and his shocked condition was too great to permit a general anaesthetic. I warned John Dominic of the consequences of delay, and of moving Leavitt to Calcutta, and he grudgingly agreed to my going ahead. I had to insert scores of stitches in a cross-patch of surgery, but when I had finished I was satisfied he would recover without too much trouble. Several months later Scott wrote to me from America to say that the wounds had healed well, and a plastic surgeon there had said the surgery could not have been improved.

The patients came from every race and class, and we became lasting friends with many of them. I very seldom had to refer any cases to Calcutta. On one of the few occasions when I had to take a seriously ill patient to Calcutta it was left to George to deal with the crisis which emerged in my absence.

Shortly after his arrival in Kalimpong from Tibet in 1950 he had become very friendly with Prince Peter of Greece and Denmark and his wife, Princess Irene, and through the social gatherings at their home met many local, national and international celebrities. Two of these had been Mr and Mrs Morgan. 'Jock' Morgan had been one of the great business tycoons during the British Raj, and like so many of that generation he was also involved in local government and charity work. When George was introduced to him and his wife at Prince Peter's he was warmly invited by the Morgans to visit them as a fellow Scot. At this time Jock Morgan and his wife were over seventy years old, Jock Morgan was retired but still director of over forty major business enterprises, and chairman of several voluntary organisations.

The Morgans had a large beautiful house set in over fourteen acres of gardens which had been planned and planted by them both as keen gardeners. They had twenty-nine servants, nine gardeners, and Mrs Morgan still worked in the garden herself for several hours each day. They dressed formally every night for dinner, and were meticulous in all social observances. The only time they were known to have deviated from fastidiously orthodox Western social behaviour was when they invited George to visit them at weekends after his football games—and he turned up covered in mud and, often, blood. This did not worry Mrs Morgan, who had his bath ready at the exact temperature for him at 5.40 p.m. so that he could appear appropriately dressed in time for drinks before dinner.

When Jock died unexpectedly in 1958 during a visit to Calcutta he was cremated there, and his ashes were brought to Kalimpong, where Mrs Morgan had them scattered on the River Teesta, flowing out of Tibet and Sikkim to the plains of India. She had asked George to be executor of their estate, together with an old Indian Army friend, Colonel Andrew Mercer, and she requested that when she died she, too, should be cremated and her ashes scattered in the same way, at the same place. When George sought to dissuade her by delicately explaining that the facilities for cremation in Kalimpong were cruder than those in Calcutta, she overcame his objections by stating firmly that she would not be in a position to be sensitive and she would appreciate his concurrence in the matter. When Colonel Mercer did not support him, George agreed with her request.

It was only a few months later that George received a telephone call, from Dr Craig in Kalimpong, to say that he was worried about Mrs Morgan's health. She had sent to him on several occasions for medicines, and when he had suggested that he pay her a visit to see what was wrong she had forbidden him to visit her. He reckoned that George was the only person who could visit her unannounced to see what was happening.

When George arrived at her home in Kalimpong he found the servants were also very worried; and when he opened the door to her room he was met by a sickening odour. Her 'Number One' house-boy told George that she had had her toe-nails cut by a travelling native chiropodist, and infection must have set in. She was too proud to acknowledge this fact by allowing Dr Craig to examine her, and her foot must have become gangrenous.

She was lying on a *chaise-longue* at the window, overlooking her beautiful garden and the backdrop of Himalayan mountains. She must have been in considerable agony, as well as personal distress at the overpowering smell, but she welcomed George graciously as always, enquiring politely after the reason for his visit. George did not prevaricate.

'I've come to take you to the hospital for Meg to look after you,' he said firmly.

'I have no intention of moving from here,' she replied equally firmly.

'You have no choice,' George stated. 'Either you call your ayah and ask her to make preparations for you to leave with me, or I will call and give orders for a chair to be brought and have you carried downstairs.'

'You will not talk to me like that in my own house,' she said furiously.

George shrugged away her anger. 'You may say what you like to me later, when you are well,' he told her. 'But I am taking you with me to Darjeeling.'

'How am I going to get there?' she conceded.

'By jeep,' George said without apology. 'I came over by jeep, and brought a mattress for you to lie on.' He gave no indication that he was aware she had never travelled in anything less than a Rolls Royce in her life.

She made no further demur, giving quiet orders to her servants, and lying down on the mattress without complaint. It was a rough journey to the hospital, but she bore it without a murmur.

When she arrived at the hospital she was seen by my Tibetan assistant, Dr Pemba. He sent for me to say drily, 'She has refused to be examined by a native.' I told her that Dr Pemba was a fully trained doctor in Western medicine, and my trusted assistant, and that she was in the hospital to be cured of a dangerous illness, not pampered in old prejudices. In any case I was going to have to leave in a few days for Calcutta with a seriously ill patient, when she would be left in Dr Pemba's care until I returned.

She responded immediately to her treatment, and despite her colonial arrogance she was well liked by the staff. She sent for the chef, instead of complaining about the food, and taught him how to cook as he had never cooked before. She was visited by the Governor of the Province, and every day the Governor's aide-de-camp brought fresh flowers for her. She was the queen of the hospital when I left for Calcutta.

In the middle of the night she died, slipping away quietly in her sleep with a fatal stroke, without even disturbing the sheets on her bed. Dr Pemba sent for George to decide what was to be done. George sent for Colonel Mercer and he asked George to make arrangements for her requested cremation as it wasn't something he could do. George knew what to do, and it had to be done before I returned from Calcutta with Mrs Morgan's sister and any of her friends.

It was monsoon time, and an inch of rain an hour was falling like a tap being opened. The cremation area was several miles away on an open promontory facing Mount Kanchenjunga. It was a Hindu religious holiday, and no priests or officials were available. George called for Loshay to prepare for a cremation, to be conducted by themselves.

As a wet and miserable dawn broke Loshay arrived at the hospital with rolls of saffron cloth, tins of ghee (a kind of butter) and cans of petrol. Mrs Morgan was rolled in the saffron cloth as a shroud and was carried to the hospital jeep. The relentless monsoon rain beat down in vertical sheets as Loshay and the hospital staff tried to get her under cover of the jeep without success; and eventually she had to be left with parts of her rain-drenched legs sticking out behind the jeep. The ghee and petrol tins were packed into Colonel Mercer's Landrover, which followed the jeep to the cremation spot.

Colonel Mercer told George that he wasn't cut out for this sort of thing and that he would look out at the mountains until it was all finished, and could George just give him a shout then? George agreed, and sat inside the jeep with his feet on the running-board watching Loshay prepare for the cremation.

He wrapped more saffron cloth on the body with liberal helpings of ghee. Then, after piling the prepared logs of wood into a pyramidal pyre, he called to George to help him place Mrs Morgan's body on top. Loshay then sloshed the cans of petrol on her body, and over the pyre, and threw on a match. The pyre blazed into life with a roar, despite the rain, and George went back to sit in the open door of the jeep.

He was sitting there reflecting on the grotesque fantasy of the elegant and fastidious Mrs Morgan, so socially correct all her life, ending it in this bizarre fashion, when she sat up in the midst of the flames. He was still staring at the sight with unbelieving eyes when Loshay casually picked up a baton of wood, swung it, and brought it with a crack against her back. She flopped back into the flames and lay still.

When he found enough voice to ask Loshay what that was all about, Loshay replied noncommittally that it happened all the time at cremations, especially with women. It was just as well that Colonel Mercer was still gazing out at the mountains with his back to the pyre, seeing nothing of the episode.

When the pyre had burned down Loshay shovelled the ashes into a brass urn. George called to Colonel Mercer that it was finished and handed him the urn. It was up to Colonel Mercer to handle the relatives and friends now. George drove madly to the airport to meet me and warn me of what had had to be done, and to say nothing to those who would be gathering at the hospital.

- 4 -
Pregnant on a Himalayan Mountain

$\mathcal{M}$eanwhile, George was at the centre of a major international *cause célèbre*. His articles about the spreading revolt and developing crisis in Tibet annoyed, then infuriated, the governments of India, Britain and America—not to mention China and Russia. Everyone believed the Chinese propaganda that 'All is peaceful in Tibet.' The representatives of the United Nations Organisation accepted the assurances of Indian Prime Minister Nehru and Chinese Premier Chou En-lai that the mutually agreed Bandung Treaty of 'The Five Principles of Peaceful Coexistence' were not only being observed, but were an accredited philosophy for resolving all sensitive political disputes, especially between neighbouring countries. Only George was writing that it was rubbish, that these so-called 'principles' were being violated every day inside Tibet, and that Prime Minister Nehru was being deliberately misled or stupidly ill-advised. India was in serious danger of being drawn into a war with China, he argued. All of this led to his being invited to give lectures and broadcasts, and to take part in debates and interviews, which led to even more publicity.

Then, as the confrontation between George and the Indian authorities was becoming critical, I received word that I was being recommended for an MBE (Member of the British Empire) award, to be presented by the Queen at Buckingham Palace, 'in recognition of your outstanding medical work in India'. Further, I was told by the British

Deputy High Commissioner, General Sir Alec Bishop, who had recommended me for the award, that the Indian Government officials had expressed the conviction that I really should have been given an Indian award rather than a British one, because it was the Indian people who had most benefited. I never learned whether they were reluctant to proceed with this because of the embarrassing contretemps over George's articles at the time! Since the MBE award was given to me as 'Dr Margaret Patterson', my professional designation of 'Miss Ingram' as a surgeon was buried in history. Anyway, whatever the protocol, it seemed I was 'Doctor Meg' to everybody.

My official popularity did not help George. He was ordered to stop publishing 'inaccurate articles' or be expelled from India—the first European in independent India to be subject to such an order. The official reason, he was given to understand, was that the material he was writing 'was prejudicial to the security interests of the Government of India'. George refused to accept either the charge or the order, and stated that he would choose to be arrested, and in a court of law countercharge that it was Prime Minister Nehru, by ignoring the Chinese activities in Tibet threatening India, who was publishing material endangering the security of India. Indian politicians and journalists who were well-disposed towards George increased their attacks on Mr Nehru's China policy. The stage was set for a major international incident.

At that point George received word from his friends inside Tibet that the Khamba revolutionaries were planning to remove the Dalai Lama from Lhasa and bring him through the Chinese armies to India. With the Dalai Lama out of danger the revolt in Tibet would be expanded and could no longer be hidden by the Chinese. In George's opinion, it would mean an inevitable confrontation between China and India, especially if the Dalai Lama asked for, and was given, sanctuary in India.

When his articles appeared there was a political outcry

in the Indian Parliament, and the Prime Minister said he would make an official statement in a day or two. Meanwhile, he reasserted: 'What is taking place in Tibet is a clash of wills, and not of arms. There is no violence in Tibet.' This report appeared in the newspapers on the same page as George's report of national revolt in Tibet.

When Mr Nehru stood up to make his announced official statement regarding his Government's action against 'Mr Patterson's inflammatory articles' the Parliamentary benches and the press gallery were packed. He said: 'I have just received a report from Lhasa that fighting has broken out there, and the Indian Consulate has been damaged in the shelling. There is no further news.' There was pandemonium as politicians demanded explanations, and journalists scrambled to reach telephones.

George heard no more about his proposed expulsion. He asked the Minister of External Affairs, Jaghat Mehta, with whom he was very friendly, whether there would be any official statement regarding his situation, and Jaghat Mehta said drily: 'George, a government might forgive you for being wrong; it is unlikely to forgive you for being right.'

However, some months later, when George asked Prime Minister Nehru for a private interview to discuss Sino-Indian issues for his book, *Peking Versus Delhi*, to everybody's surprise he agreed and talked pleasantly and informatively with George, even where they disagreed on the status of Tibet. From then on it was generally assumed among officials that all was forgiven, if not forgotten.

My appointment as Medical Adviser to the Sherpa Mountaineering Association had come through Sherpa Tenzing, the conqueror of Mount Everest with Sir Edmund Hillary, whom George had known for several years. I had treated his two daughters, Pem Pem and Nima, on several occasions. Like Tenzing, they were both skilled mountaineers, and while still in their early teens had held the world record for being the youngest women to climb the highest mountains.

During that tense winter of 1958–59 building up to George's order of expulsion and the Dalai Lama's escape, Tenzing asked me if I would like to join them in the first International Women's Climbing Expedition to one of the major Himalayan peaks. He was going with them, and Pem Pem and Nima had been invited to go as official members of the expedition. When I said that I had no experience of mountain climbing he said I would not need it, that all I would need was the ability to function as a doctor at the base camp at 18,000 feet. If I agreed, he and some Sherpas would take me out on a preliminary climb with Pem Pem and Nima to acclimatise me on a nearby 22,000-foot mountain.

Of course, I agreed. My assistant doctor, Tsewang Pemba, the first Tibetan to graduate in Western medicine in Cambridge and London, also wanted to take his Fellowship in Surgery in England, and I was training him with this in mind. He was perfectly capable of looking after the hospital in my absence.

George was very envious, but although Tenzing tried to get permission for him to go with us, George's provocative articles about Tibet, and the possibility of revolt there leading to outright war between India and China, had brought him into disfavour with the Indian authorities and they would not permit him to go with us.

The first several days of climbing were an intoxicating experience—almost literally. For, while I had become accustomed to living at 9,000 feet above sea level in Darjeeling so that I was unaware of the effects of altitude, our steady climb upwards above this height created the usual light-headed euphoria as the oxygen in the atmosphere diminished. I had been asked by the Director of the Himalayan Mountaineering Institute, Major Gyan Singh, to keep detailed records of the effects of high altitude on all members of the party, and I added my personal experience to this as well.

It was indescribably beautiful as day by day we passed through spectacular vistas of valleys, forests, mountains and snows, with Sherpa and Lepcha villages perched on the shoulders of ridges under the towering Himalayan peaks. The Sherpas—every one a famous name (Gompu, the one assigned to look after me personally, would even surpass Tenzing by climbing Everest twice in the next few years)— were unfailingly cheerful and attentive. At meal times fires were lit, meals cooked and presented in no time at all, and they would talk and sing around the fire until it was time to sleep under a blue-black sky filled with scintillating stars.

At 13,000 feet I began to suffer from altitude sickness and Tenzing ordered Gompu and Loshay, George's servant who had insisted on coming to look after me, to remain with me at that altitude for the next forty-eight hours to allow acclimatisation, while the others continued the climb.

The next morning I felt wonderful again, well enough to countermand Tenzing's orders and insist that Gompu, Loshay and I push ahead and try to catch up quickly on the others. All that day I knew a physical and mental euphoria such as I had never experienced before (although George had warned me about the dangers as well as the delights of the altitude reaction), and I strode ahead at a reckless pace. At 17,000 feet I suddenly became acutely ill again, and Gompu and Loshay had to support and almost carry me for the remaining one thousand feet or so to the base camp.

Tenzing had been exploring the approach to the summit prior to the final planned assault, but he found the weather conditions deteriorating so badly that he decided against climbing any higher. While I rested and recovered at the base camp the others climbed some of the lower peaks, and at some points crossed the border into Tibet. I was disappointed not to be with them, but I had signed a document before leaving Darjeeling in which I promised that I would not cross the border. As it was, I was the first foreigner in ten years to be given permission to enter that sensitive area.

After an equally spectacular descent, when we returned to Darjeeling I continued to be nauseated at intervals, and I asked George if this was customary when returning from high altitudes. He thought it unlikely, for his own experience was that it usually disappeared when he returned to 10,000 feet.

Then, one day while I was doing a critical operation on a local doctor's wife, a repeat of two previously failed operations by other gynaecologists, and the doctor was present, I was suddenly acutely embarrassed to be sick at the operating table. I was forced to think the unthinkable: was I pregnant? Without saying anything to George I sent a urine specimen for laboratory analysis. It seemed wishful thinking in view of the many assertions by medical specialists that I was unlikely to have children after my operations. We were so certain that I could not have children that we were seriously considering adopting three Tibetan refugee children.

When the laboratory report came back it was positive. I was pregnant. I told George, who was overjoyed, and at a public gathering when Tenzing was present he made the announcement—and added that, if the child were born with black hair and slanting eyes, he would know who the father was! Tenzing hugely enjoyed this joke at his expense, and was amused when for some time after this he was teased about his 'high altitude fertility clinic'. I never got to join the Women's Climbing Expedition after all. I was otherwise engaged.

Because of my previous history of radical surgery it was decided that I ought to have the baby under skilled surgical supervision, and I arranged to go for the birth to my old hospital in Aberdeen where I had done some of my early training. There our first son, Lorne, was born on November 27th, 1959—without slanting eyes or dark hair! He had grey-blue eyes like his father, and auburn hair like me. Nevertheless, he continued to be a favourite of Tenzing, who gave him a present of a silver-and-jade Tibetan drinking bowl.

The national and international publicity over Tibet had

brought George many requests for help from other small nations and groups, among them the Nagas from north-east India near the frontier with Burma. He had met some of the leaders when visiting a missionary friend, Walter Corlett of the Carey Baptist Church, in Calcutta. The Nagas had been a fearsome head-hunting tribe who had never been conquered from the time of Ptolemy; even during the period of British rule in India they had not been conquered, and the British authorities had agreed to let their headmen be responsible for good order in their territories. About a hundred years before, some American Baptists had gone to evangelise them and they responded in a remarkable manner, and it was now reckoned that over seventy per cent of the Naga people were committed evangelical Christians.

With Indian independence, despite assurances from Britain, the Nagas were 'handed over' to the incoming Indian Government. At first they simply protested at this breach of agreement (in which they were supported by no less than Mahatma Ghandi), then when their protests were ignored, and the Indian authorities introduced measures replacing the Naga Christian leaders with Hindu civil servants, they resorted to rebellion against the Indian armed police. When it looked as if the Indian police and officials were going to be swept away the Indian Government sent in their army, closed off the whole area in Upper Assam, forbade the media to visit, and enforced their rule.

This was the situation that the Naga leaders whom George met in Calcutta wanted him to investigate and report. He began to do so—and again came into conflict with Indian authorities.

However, before he became too involved we were faced with the need to make important personal decisions. To complete his new and most ambitious political book, *Peking Versus Delhi*, George needed to get to better libraries than he could find in India. And I had to decide whether I was going to renew my contract with the Tea Planters' Hospital. My assistant, Dr Pemba, had successfully obtained his

Fellowship of the Royal College of Surgeons in London—he won the top prize with the highest marks of all the applicants from all over the world—and he wanted to remain at the Tea Planters' Hospital where he could treat his fellow Tibetans. I was very touched by Dr Pemba's statement regarding working with me, when he said, 'One of the greatest things I learned from Dr Patterson was that she made each patient feel as if she had all the time in the world for him or her, and yet she moved through a large number of patients at an incredible rate.'

Before returning to Scotland, we decided to use up our accumulated local leave by going to an isolated beach resort on the north-east coast of India, for our first holiday since our honeymoon seven years earlier. On our way through Calcutta, I insisted on George seeing a physician friend, Dr Hans Hahndel, because of recent abdominal discomfort and diarrhoea. Hans ordered an urgent barium meal X-ray. We stared at the films together: it was the largest gastric ulcer I had ever seen that wasn't a cancer of the stomach—and my professional specialty was gastroenterology.

Hans ordered me to go on holiday as planned with Lorne—at that time one year old—while he admitted George to hospital in Calcutta and kept him under very heavy sedation, on a diet of only crackers and milk, for the next ten days. It was not a pleasant experience being on my own, and not knowing what was happening to George back in Calcutta. I also nearly drowned during my stay! There was a huge surf and it looked so inviting to dive into that I did so, even though not an expert swimmer. What I was not aware of was the powerful undercurrent which dragged me further and further down, and I only just managed to struggle to the surface and back to the shore.

When I returned to Calcutta, Hans did a second barium meal. To our delight, George's ulcer had healed to less than half its original size, which meant that it was not malignant, and convalescence could continue at home. We left that same afternoon for Darjeeling, but spending the night with very close friends who lived in the foothills. Ron was a Scottish tea-planter, and his wife Deki was a charming Sikkimese girl who had worked as my secretary before her marriage, and lived with us during that time since her own parents lived in Sikkim.

It is an established habit in India for servants to bring morning tea to guests in bed; but Deki, with Eastern courtesy, decided to bring it herself, that being an expression of honour to welcome guests. We were just reunited after George's stay in hospital, and after a good sleep, we were enjoying our first blissful intimacy in ten days—when Deki walked into the room carrying the tea-tray. She almost dropped it as she turned scarlet with embarrassment, having thought that we would still be asleep. That morning produced Sean nine months later and also finalised our decision to return to Scotland.

Sean now takes delight in teasing Deki that he 'was born in sin, shapen in iniquity, and conceived in public!'

On our return to England, George was to join Guy Wint at St Antony's in Oxford, to complete his book, and also to look into the possibilities of taking up politics instead of writing.

When our second son, Sean, was born on September 12th, 1961—the eighth anniversary of our wedding—we found a small isolated house on the lovely Mull of Kintyre, in the West Highlands of Scotland, and George was accepted as Liberal candidate for the Edinburgh West constituency. For the first time since I was married—since I graduated—I had no medical responsibilities. I was a housewife, a mother of two small children, and my only extra-domestic commitment was to attend, and sometimes to address, some of George's constituency meetings as a politician's wife.

But it did not last long. I had said to George that I didn't think he was meant to be a politician, despite his obvious writing and verbal skills; and, sure enough, within a few months he was recalled to London by Guy Wint and

David Astor, the editor of the *Observer*, to investigate the worsening Naga situation in India. The underground President of the Nagas, A. Z. Phizo, had now arrived in London, and David Astor wanted George to interview him.

Phizo came to live with us for several weeks while George had long in-depth talks with him, but George concluded that he was not a genuine informant, because there were too many discrepancies in his accounts of events. George advised that he send for some of his colleagues, military and political, to give some force to his statements. We moved to a flat in London, and George arranged to pursue research for his book at Oxford.

George and Meg outside Buckingham Palace on the day she received the MBE from Her Majesty the Queen.
1962

I was beginning to feel the strain of this hectic existence. When we were in India I had had servants to look after the household affairs, and a wonderful amah—children's nanny—to look after Lorne. Then there was always Loshay, who was for ever anticipating our needs. George had found Loshay a job in the Homes, and he was now happily married in Kalimpong.

I enjoyed being with the children, but the household chores overwhelmed me. When visitors occupied George in endless discussions about politics or Scriptures, or, even worse, when he was away in Oxford or elsewhere, I found myself in the unusual situation of finding difficulty in coping with circumstances. Suddenly, my life seemed to have disengaged from the driving, exciting purpose of the past.

Then we had a letter from some of our Tibetan official friends in Kalimpong to say that they wished to come to England and the United States to make their country's plight known to the world. One of them was Tibet's leading Cabinet Minister, Surkhang Shapay, who was one of the chief architects of the Tibetan revolt, and his wife, brother and two teenage children. The other was Yangpel Pangdatshang, the Tibetan Trade Minister, whose two brothers had looked after George during his three years in Tibet; he had a new young wife, a small son—and a family retainer.

While George was arranging for them to come to England we received word from the Pakistan Embassy in London that two Naga generals, two Naga politicians, and 153 Naga soldiers had arrived in East Pakistan, after a highly publicised journey shooting their way through the Indian Army mobilised to stop them, 'looking for George Patterson'. So George had to fly to East Pakistan to make arrangements for the two generals, Kaito and Mowu, and the two politicians, to come to England to present their case against India.

Both groups of Tibetan and Naga revolutionary leaders, including those with families, wanted to be with us in our home rather than in hotels, so we bought several mattresses and juggled arrangements to fit. Life became even more hectic as George arranged for them to be heard by officials, media and academics. While he was away in Oxford or elsewhere with the Naga leaders I was at home trying to cope with the remaining Nagas at home, attending to the children, shopping and all the usual demands of a harassed mother.

On one occasion, on an icy winter's day, when I had taken the children on to Clapham Common, three-year-old Lorne was walking alongside the pond when he slipped on the ice and fell into the water, which was a few feet deep at that place. I quickly left one-year-old Sean in the pram and slid down the icy slope into the freezing cold water to rescue Lorne. I managed to pull him out with a struggle, and both of us were soaked, Lorne worse than me. I quickly wrapped him in my coat and sat him in the pram with Sean. I ran for home, desperately looking for a taxi.

It was amazing that, while there were few people on the Common, not one of the people on the streets or in their cars, seeing a soaking wet mother with a soaking wet child wrapped in her coat, on a cold winter's day, frantically hurrying along the pavement, offered to help. I had to walk the whole way home, but the kindly Nagas helped to get Lorne into a hot bath, and made me hot tea. Neither of us suffered any serious consequences from the incident.

David Astor, Guy Wint and the Reverend Michael Scott, with George as first Director, set up an organisation, the International Committee for the Study of Group Rights—later to be called 'The Minority Rights Group'—to represent the interests of oppressed and exploited minority peoples such as the Nagas and the Tibetans before the United Nations.

Meanwhile I was pregnant again, while the frantic events spun around me. The Nagas and the Tibetans—men as well as women—were wonderfully supportive. Cabinet Minister Surkhang Shapay did the shopping. His brother,

General Surkhang, helped with the washing up. The women looked after the children. The Naga generals sang Christian hymns and Naga battle songs as bedtime lullabies to our wide-eyed boys.

When, despite all their efforts, their activities looked like ending in frustration and despair in the face of the disinterest of Western governments, they pressured George somehow to publicise their predicament again as he had done in the past. George was reluctant to get involved personally in a situation which must eventually lead him back to the East. But he arranged for a well-known television producer, Adrian Cowell, and cameraman, Chris Menges, to meet with the Nagas and Tibetans to discuss the possibility of a series to help publicise their situations.

George's reluctance arose from a spiritual crisis which we were going through at that time. Our respective individual activities were multiplying, but instead of them overlapping, and integrating, as they had done in the past, giving us confidence that we were in the purpose of God and moving forward to a divinely ordained goal, we now seemed to be forever chasing just to keep up with demanding daily events. Somewhere along the way the golden light had gone out of our relationship, and we had become tired, numb, irritable—near strangers. I saw no end to the political demands being made on George, and the domestic demands being made on me, with the consequent further deterioration in what had been a romance of unsurpassable promise. I wanted a more ordered life, a more structured domestic arrangement, a more secure existence. It was all very well discussing plans for rebellions and media projects in restaurants and offices; it was a different matter altogether struggling to get on to a crowded bus with a pram, on a wet day, with two tired, hungry and wet children.

George's mockery and satire, which he had always used as a relatively harmless weapon to attack social, political and ecclesiastical pretensions and hypocrisies, was deepening under the constant pressures into bitterness and cynicism. At forty-three years of age, with a deep and genuine Christian commitment to help the poor, the sick, the exploited, the oppressed, he saw his former friends with houses, cars, settled jobs and apparently tranquil lives. We went from one financial crisis to another, were continually involved in arguments and discussions with families and friends about our way of life, while we tried to solve the problems of warring nations in an atmosphere of James Bond-like conspiracies.

George's reaction was even stronger than mine. He wanted to give up everything and retire to Scotland and write at leisure. I would have settled for a more prosaic arrangement of each finding a steady job and an 'ordinary' lifestyle. We decided to go to George's brother, Bill's, farm in Scotland to sort out our life.

We lived in a caravan. It rained every day. We trudged through mud. Clothes never dried. The 'simplicities' were even more intolerable than our previous complexities. We reached the depths of strained relationships, with angry words and hurtful attitudes, before we broke and clung to each other in forgiveness and tears. Out of this battering on the anvil of God we prayed that He would forge us anew into instruments of His purpose.

It was back to square one. If God wanted George in Tibet and Asia risking death, with me home with the children, and no future, that was what we had accepted with such glad abandon—without the blessing of children—ten years before. We nerved ourselves for the battle again.

George told Adrian and Chris that he was prepared to join them in making a series of television films about oppressed small nations in Asia: the Tibetans against the Chinese, the Nagas against India, the Shans against Burma, and Taiwan against China. The Nagas returned to Nagaland to make preparations for the television team's arrival. We sold off what possessions we had to help pay for the series, for only Granada Television was prepared to take the series—and they had so little hope of success that they were only willing to put up a small amount of money. I moved into a small cottage in Sussex with the children and the Tibetans. George gave me two hundred pounds, and a new copy of a will. That was all we owned in the world. Even the insurance policy was turned in. David Astor turned down an exclusive series for the *Observer*, because, as a friend, he felt he should discourage George from a project that looked like certain death.

They were going behind the Chinese Army lines inside Tibet after climbing 20,000-foot Himalayan mountains in Nepal; they were going behind Indian Army lines in Nagaland, where Naga rebels were being shot at sight; they were going behind Burmese Army lines in the Shan states, where there were several renegade armies; and they were going to try to land on the Chinese mainland with the Chinese Nationalist guerrillas.

Six weeks before George left on the trip, which was expected to take about eighteen months, our daughter was born, on December 23rd, 1963. We called her Myrrh, partly because she was due to be born on Christmas Day, partly because of the bitterness of the experience through which we had just passed, and partly because it was also the rare perfume which had been presented to Jesus at His birth and His death. It was all that we had to offer to God.

I had a few letters from George from India, and Nepal. Then, suddenly, a cable arrived from Nepal asking if I would be interested in working as a surgeon in the United Mission Hospital in Kathmandu, the capital of Nepal. I could scarcely believe what I was reading. Was there no limit to my husband's madness? In any case, I was just recovering from a bout of viral pneumonia, and Sean had dislocated his neck while bouncing on the bed. I told George this in a reasonably moderate reply.

Another letter from George arrived, explaining that the United Mission Hospital had just lost five surgeons through retirement, sickness, leave and death; and that Dr Anderson, who knew me, had asked George if I would consider a six-month appointment.

I sent a cable to him agreeing to go, and had a nightmarish time trying to get our belongings into storage, obtain new passports with the children's names, typhoid and cholera injections for everybody, then get the children to the airport and onto the plane. I was looking forward with more than eager anticipation to George meeting us when we got to Nepal.

There was no sign of George at Kathmandu airport, but a Chinese woman friend from our Darjeeling days, who was now living in Kathmandu, met us and said that George had left Kathmandu a week or so before and would be back soon. I doubted it, for I knew where George was going and she obviously did not. She was about to be married to an American embassy official, and I knew George would not be saying anything other than generalities.

I had been given a beautiful bungalow belonging to the British Council Director, who was on leave; but it was seven miles from the hospital, six miles from the nearest main road, and there was no telephone and no transport. It had been arranged that the hospital ambulance would pick me up at eight o'clock every morning, and take me back home at six in the evening.

In the meantime, the children—aged four years, two years and five months—were left in the care of male Nepali servants, who spoke no English. I telephoned friends in Calcutta and asked if they could find an English-speaking amah, and put her on the plane to Kathmandu the next day if possible. Two weeks later I discovered that she was a sadist, and that the children lived in fear of her.

With George still not appearing, everyone—including the British Ambassador, Mr (later Sir, and Head of MI5 Security Service) Anthony Duff, and his wife, Polly—were very kind to me. Unfortunately, I had to be very careful what I said about George and his possible whereabouts. In his usual journalistic way George had left a smokescreen of rumours as a cover for his true intentions.

One of the people he had met in providing his smokescreen was Juddhabir Lama, the personal assistant to the Nepalese Prime Minister. We had got to know the Lama family while we were in Darjeeling. They had arrived at the hospital late one night, bringing one of their sons, Juddhabir's brother, Amir, in a moribund state. To save his life I had to operate immediately and needed blood for transfusion during the operation. It was impossible to find enough blood at such short notice late at night, and there was no blood bank nearer than Calcutta, some 500 miles away. Fortunately, his blood group was the same as George's, so George gave a direct blood transfusion while Amir was being prepared for surgery. Amir was so nearly dead that I dared not go ahead without an initial transfusion.

A rapid incision produced a fountain of blood. I filtered the several pints of blood which had been lost into Amir's abdominal cavity, and put it directly back into his vein. But we had no suction apparatus, and as soon as I released pressure from the bleeding area, blood filled the wound, so it was impossible to visualise the source of the bleeding. It was obviously a losing battle . . .

My thoughts flashed back twelve years to an occasion when I was assisting Mr Norman Tanner, the world-famous gastric and oesophageal surgeon, in St James Hospital, Balham, London, at a complicated portocaval anastomosis. Suddenly, a jet of blood shot into the air. Mr Tanner calmly packed the bleeding area with a large gauze pack and closed the wound. Forty-eight hours later he removed half the pack and the remainder in another twenty-four hours. To my astonishment, there was no bleeding and the patient went home, seemingly no worse of the procedure.

I repeated that technique on Amir with similar results. Six years later, when we met again in Kathmandu, he was in excellent health and had never discovered the cause of his emergency illness. The family was very grateful to us for saving Amir's life, and George was considered a 'blood

brother'. Now, both Juddhabir and Amir held influential
positions in the Nepalese government in Kathmandu, and
George had spent time with them before slipping secretly
into Tibet. But I had to meet them, too, and not give
anything away.

I had just decided after five weeks that I must tell the
Ambassador what I knew of George's plans, because he
might have been captured, imprisoned or killed, when one
morning the door opened and they were there.

I hardly recognised him. He had lost over thirty
pounds, and he was as slim and deeply tanned as when we
had first met. Adrian and Chris were the same. They were
triumphant, for they had crossed the Himalayas with a
Tibetan guerrilla group and had filmed them in action
against the Chinese occupation army inside Tibet, and were
therefore able to prove that the much-vaunted Chinese
military control over Tibet was a myth. They had gone
straight to the Kathmandu airport and had got the films out
of the country before anyone could suspect anything—even
that they were back in Kathmandu.

It was just as well, for when George informed the
Ambassador what they had done, and what they had found
out about the Khamba guerrilla raids over the borders, the
Ambassador asked if he could inform the King about it.
George agreed, and the King was furious with his Cabinet
ministers, who had not informed him of the serious
situation. They, with their jobs in jeopardy, thought that the
films were still in George's possession, and that if they could
be obtained and destroyed, they could justify themselves
before the King and save their jobs. So they sent police,
security and high officials to interrogate and threaten him.
Adrian and Chris had left for Calcutta, by arrangement, and
George stayed behind to handle the repercussions. But the
officials could not obtain a warrant to search the house, for it
had diplomatic immunity as a British Council residence.

Later, we learned that at least two of the officials who
came to the house were armed. They had sat with their

hands on their revolvers throughout their visit, in the expectation that if they found out George had the films they were going to take them from him by force, if necessary.

When George made arrangements to leave Nepal a few days later, the children and I went with him to the airport. There was a large turnout there as a high American diplomat was leaving on the same plane. George had advised the press corps that he was likely to be stopped, and there were more media people around George than there were around the diplomat. No action was taken against him at the counter, but as he walked to the exit a plain-clothes official stopped him. George shrugged him off. The media crowded around. The children were wide-eyed and white-faced as they watched their father.

George moved out onto the apron to walk to the plane, and the official called to the two Gurkha soldiers standing at the barrier. They drew their curved *kukris* and presented the bare blades to stop George moving through. George stopped at the swords, with his chest touching them. The media shouted for him to stand there while they took films and photographs.

Eventually, George had to withdraw. But he refused to leave the airport with anybody until he had spoken to the British Embassy. He was unable to contact the Ambassador but the First Secretary said to wait there until he arrived. After a great deal of argument it was agreed that George could return to our British Council residence, but the authorities would have to provide an official explanation for their handling of a respected British journalist. It was the last throw of frustrated officialdom, and they had to let George leave the country.

Once again I was on my own, and I settled down to my daily routine of seeing about a hundred outpatients a day, with a half-day list of surgical operations. Fortunately with a new amah the children were now enjoying themselves in Nepal. But the repercussions of George's trip into Tibet were to remain for a long time; among them, several top officials lost their jobs, and mountaineering expeditions were refused permission to climb in the Himalayas for the next several years.

Two months later I received a letter from him from Hong Kong. They had decided for political reasons not to do the film of the Nagas, because India had agreed to enter into delicate peace negotiations. They had continued with the Shan assignment instead. George had gone ahead of Adrian and Chris to Hong Kong and Taiwan to make arrangements for the other films.

Would I like to join him in Hong Kong? And would I be prepared to work in a Chinese charity hospital that was in desperate need of a general surgeon?

- 5 -
An Unexpected Medical Discovery in Hong Kong

*I*in September 1964, I flew into Hong Kong just as the sun was setting, and millions of lights were flickering on all over the colony. I had never seen anything so fairy-tale beautiful.

The plane came in on a wide sweep over the many small, darkening islands in the green-blue sea, passed between the high mountains sheltering the world-famous harbour and then, incredibly, approached the airport between and just above the multitudinous, towering skyscrapers that covered the city in gigantic caverns.

George was at the airport this time, and I fell into his arms, choking with gratitude and relief. I had been so fearful that I might be left on my own again in another strange city.

We drove back through the dwarfing residential and office skyscrapers, ablaze at street level with every kind of coloured light, and lined with a mind-bewildering variety of goods in the myriad small shops. We left the city of Kowloon behind and crossed the harbour to the city of Victoria, standing at the rails of the cross-harbour ferry with the excited children to watch the oncoming sweep of lights on Hong Kong Island. Then we drove to the far side of the island, to Repulse Bay, where George had found a flat and a delightful cook and his wife-amah as a nanny for the children, A-chu and Lindy. We were all together again.

Our flat in Repulse Bay overlooked the wide sweep of the South China Sea, and was part of the home of Roger and

Margaret Lobo. Roger was a businessman who was also a member of the Legislative Council of the Government, and Margaret was a lovely friend, with eleven children of her own, who helped me settle into Hong Kong. With Margaret as a neighbour, and Lindy a delightful Christian amah, I had no worries about the children. And George was writing at home most of the time, anyway.

Meg with Lorne, Myrrh and Sean, in a flat rented from Sir Roger and Lady Margaret Lobo, Repulse Bay, Hong Kong.
1964

The Chinese charity hospital, Tung Wah, where I was to work was one of a group of three hospitals—the Tung Wah Group of Hospitals, with a total of two thousand beds, the largest in Asia—and it had 850 beds. I was Head of Surgery. Although it had been started as a charity with individual and institutional donations, in recent years the Hong Kong Government had provided huge subsidies so that the facilities were as good as an average hospital in Britain. They were certainly an advance on any of the places in which I had worked in India or Nepal.

I was the only European doctor in the three hospitals, but all the doctors and nurses spoke English, and I only required an interpreter for some of my lectures and for interviewing patients, the majority of whom did not speak English. The English language was a mandatory study in all Hong Kong schools, so everybody except new refugees from mainland China spoke it. After a while I learned enough Cantonese to handle them on my own.

I could not have done any of the work without the help of our Chinese amah, Lindy. She was an absolute treasure, and the children loved her. Myrrh especially was like one of her own children, for the boys were at school during the day. Myrrh learned to use the Chinese chopsticks and enjoy Chinese food before learning to use Western utensils and eat Western food.

But it wasn't easy being away from the children all day, much as I loved surgery—as on the day when we had to employ a temporary ayah to look after the children. She took them to the nearby beach, crowded with swimmers, and the two boys went into the sea, wearing egg-like floaters strapped on to their backs. Three-year-old Sean was swimming so easily that he thought he could do it without the floater; the amah didn't see him take it off and he was unable to get his head above the water again. Five-year-old Lorne phoned me at the hospital to say that he had found Sean drowned; he pulled him out of the water, got some adults to take him to the lifeguards who immediately started resuscitation until the ambulance arrived—and so saved his life. Lorne ran home alone to phone me. Sean had been taken to the large Queen Mary Hospital. The agony of that thirty-minute drive to the hospital will never leave me.

By the time I arrived there, he had recovered consciousness, but remembered nothing of what had happened, not even the long ambulance journey. The next week I started all three of them on swimming lessons!

On Sundays when Lindy and A-Chu had their day off, and if George was not available to look after the children, I took them to the hospital with me if I was called in to do emergency surgery. We dressed them up in cap, surgical mask and gown, their little feet lost in the adult theatre boots. They soon learned the principles of sterility and 'non-touch'. My anaesthetists were wonderfully kind and patient with them, would fetch stools for them to stand on so they could see everything that was going on, and often let them compress the re-breathing bag. Fortunately, they have only happy memories of these occasions.

The Hong Kong Chinese—98 per cent of the population—were mostly from the Cantonese-speaking province of Kwangtung, about twenty miles away up the peninsula from Kowloon, with a smattering from Fukien and Shanghai.

Hong Kong was an amazing place. In places—such as in the Central District business area, with its imposing modern, multi-storey skyscraper offices and glittering shopping arcades—it was wholly Western. And elsewhere—as in the Hollywood area to the east of the island, with its network of small shops in narrow lanes, where I worked in the Tung Wah Hospital, or in the rice-fields and villages of the New Territories between Kowloon and the Chinese border—it was wholly Chinese.

The pace of life was incredible. The four million inhabitants lived in a less than thirteen-square-mile area of Kowloon and Hong Kong, from among the many scattered islands making up the colony. They poured out of the high-rise tenements in a clean and well-dressed flood every morning, crowding the pavements shoulder-to-shoulder with bright-eyed sophisticated elegance as they hurried to offices and factories. Even after office hours the pavements were filled with strolling people visiting shops, markets and restaurants in noisy, friendly groups. The roads were jammed with jostling cars and gleaming limousines, weaving between the clanging, packed tramcars, nose to tail in search of parking places.

Many Chinese held down two jobs, setting up stalls in

the narrow side streets or open markets; or even using their small flats as temporary workshops, where they assembled toys for manufacturers under sub-contracts. The schools were in such demand that they operated on a two-shift basis, from six a.m. to two p.m., and the second lot from two p.m. to ten p.m.

The Chinese studied hard, worked hard and played hard, and the consequences were evident in the economic miracle that was Hong Kong. Refugees who arrived penniless from the Chinese Communist mainland to live in the corrugated-iron shacks quickly found work and new living quarters, and within a few years were well-to-do businessmen—many of them even millionaires.

But the price that Hong Kong paid for its bondage to Mammon, its worship of money and materialism, was high in physical and social sickness. Almost sixty per cent of Hong Kong's population was under twenty-five years of age; over seventy per cent of all crime was committed by youths under twenty-five; and over seventy per cent of those were drug addicts, most of them members of the sinister secret societies.

The soulless, crowded, high-rise buildings, the ruthless pursuit of wealth and status and possessions, the lack of privacy and community life and involvement, the pressures to find schooling and pass-marks and advancement—with an inadequate, almost nonexistent, safety net of social and medical welfare—had its inevitable moral and physical consequences. Crime and vice and corruption spread their merciless tentacles everywhere behind the oriental splendour, manipulated by the dreaded Chinese 'Triads', the secret societies which had controlled Hong Kong's affairs since its birth a century before. It was reckoned that ten per cent of Hong Kong's population were members of one or other of these secret societies, from business tycoons to boatmen.

All of this fascinating *mélange* was brought home to me right from the start of my arrival in Hong Kong. George had arranged for our Tibetan Trade Minister friend, Yangpel Pangdatshang, to come to Hong Kong to settle some business affairs. He introduced him to one of the leading lawyers to handle the matter, Brian Tisdall, then George left for Taiwan to make arrangements for their television trip with the Nationalist guerrillas to the mainland of China. When he returned to Hong Kong, Brian Tisdall informed George that Yangpel and his family had disappeared, and after the most intense police and security search he was never found. Many months later he surfaced in China, and was afterwards murdered in Tibet. His brother in India offered high rewards for information, the family initiated high-level enquiries, George used all of his contacts—and it all added up to a Hong Kong kidnapping in broad daylight that was never revealed at any level.

At this time George was also investigating the drug traffic in Hong Kong, for the second part of their television documentary, *The Opium Trail*; the first part had been completed in the Shan states of Burma—'the Golden Triangle'—and Thailand. When this was completed George decided to stay on in Hong Kong. He had been asked to write a book about the reported Russian and Chinese confrontation on their mutual borders[1], and a book about Christianity in Communist China[2]. But, also, in their film investigations the television team had found that the seven hundred pounds of raw opium being grown annually in the Shan states, when processed into heroin and sold in Hong Kong to the Mafia agents from Europe and the United States, generated some US$2 billion—and these profits were even more astronomical when the heroin reached the West. George wanted to know what happened to such huge profits in Asia: who was being bribed to do what?

That was when the telephone harassment campaign was launched against us. The telephone would ring at irregular

---

[1] *The Unquiet Frontier* (Dragonfly Books, 1965).

[2] *Christianity in Communist China* (Word Inc., 1968).

intervals all through each night, with either lewd or obscene messages to me, or threatening silence if George answered. When we reported it to the telephone company, then to the police, no action was taken—until George went to the Commissioner of Police. He said they could do very little and suggested changing the number—something that was of no use to me as a surgeon on constant call, or to George as a sceptical journalist knowing how easy it would be for any harasser to obtain a new number in Hong Kong.

Eventually, George took matters into his own hands, selecting a few highly placed criminals and intelligence agents whom he knew, and informing them that he would release certain important information which he had regarding their activities, and which he was withholding for professional reasons, if the harassment did not cease. Somewhere, and with someone, he must have hit it right, for we were not bothered again.

In the charity Tung Wah Hospital I saw the detritus of Hong Kong society from another angle. The sick who could not afford the high charges of doctors or other hospitals, the unwanted members of families too busy or too ambitious to care, the mentally and physically handicapped for whom the Government made no provision—all came to us. Many of them used opiates either to dull the pain of living, or as a form of Chinese medicine, and I had to make an allowance for this in all of my diagnoses, before and after operations. Opiates were easily available in Hong Kong, and there was no stigma attached to the indulgence; a packet of heroin cost less than a packet of cigarettes. At one time I counted eleven out of the fourteen patients in one of my surgical wards were on some form of opiates.

My work in Tung Wah had much less extemporised drama than my previous hospitals, and my daily surgery lists were the same as in most other hospitals. I had more lectures to deliver, and more aspiring surgeons to train for their Fellowships.

George and I were so deeply immersed in our

respective writing and hospital work, so different yet so fascinatingly related at times, that it came as quite a surprise when George was approached by the newly established Hong Kong Trade Development Council to design and prepare new publications for them. Apparently, when the Council was formed the Director asked Derek Davies, the editor of the *Far Eastern Economic Review* and a good friend of ours, to recommend a professional writer and journalist to do the job, and he had suggested George. At first George was reluctant to take it on as he knew nothing about trade, but he was persuaded by the Assistant Director of the Council, Len Dunning, to do it. Among other things the generous salary meant that we could change accommodation, and we moved from Repulse Bay to the nearby fishing village of Stanley, where a ground-floor beach flat belonging to a colleague of George's was available.

George had agreed to work for the Trade Development Council for a year, but to complete the new journal, *Hong Kong Enterprise*, and other publications, he stayed on for another year. This provided us with paid leave to visit Britain in 1968, and we chose to travel back via the United States. George had been asked to do a lecture tour there following on the televising of the films and the publication of his books. The youth protest movements, and the explosion of the rock music phenomenon of the Beatles, the Rolling Stones, 'The Who', and other bands, with their emphasis on drugs, the occult and revolutionary social changes, had created interest in George and his experiences.

George had also been invited to talk with Christian leaders following on the publication of his book, *Christianity in Communist China*, and articles he had written entitled *Communications and the Christian Gospel*. The latter had arisen out of his investigation of the recent development of satellite broadcasting and its significance for developing countries in Asia. George's theory was that, just as Christianity expanded in the nineteenth and early twentieth centuries under the umbrella of medicine and education and a beneficent colonialism, in the more nationalist late twentieth and twenty-first centuries the expansion should be under the umbrella of the media.

Through his many Chinese and Asian friends— especially the Chinese journalists Jack Chow and Timothy Yu—he had been excited by the emergence of powerful Christian indigenous movements in Asia. These had many wealthy and influential Christian businessmen as members, who were disillusioned with the restraints and weaknesses of the orthodox Christian denominational institutions. They were not inclined to put the tithes of their money into ecclesiastical buildings or traditionalist practices, and were exploring the possibilities of establishing Christian banks to fund Christian enterprises. When George and Timothy and Jack proposed taking a major stake in an Asian satellite system in order to have a say in the content of programmes, they heartily approved.

Timothy Yu set out to establish a Communications Centre in Hong Kong to train all forms of media expertise, so that Asian nationals would not go to the USA for the training and then remain there in lucrative jobs. George was to explore the possibility of interest and participation with finance or expertise among Christians in the United States and Europe.

Unfortunately, while there was great interest and enthusiasm it was mostly directed towards the potential for extended fundamentalist sermonising along the lines already being used by television evangelists, and not towards issues of social change based on Christian values. He spent a frustrating eighteen months flying backwards and forwards between the East and the West, while he and his friends tried to arrange a multimillion-dollar international deal with Asian Governments and Western finance.

The money from jobs and books and lecture tours had rapidly disappeared, and gifts from families and friends were quickly being used up in following up promising opportunities. These were tantalising enough to keep them trying in the face of monumental discouragements and lack of daily living expenses. I rarely saw George between 1968 and 1970. He would pass through Hong Kong on his way to Thailand, Singapore, Indonesia and the Philippines, and I would see him for a few days. He felt he was on the edge of fulfilment of his great vision to change the world, and no sacrifice was too great to accomplish this.

Meanwhile, during his brief stopovers in Hong Kong, George would call on the shopkeepers and the authorities to plead with them to hold off their pressing demands for payment of bills and taxes. I had to keep the family on my meagre charity salary—which was exactly half the amount paid to my male counterparts in the hospital, and a fraction of what I could have made in private practice—and for a time this was only enough to feed us on soup and crackers. I don't know what I would have done if it had not been for the kindness of our local Chinese Communist grocer, who uncomplainingly kept me in provisions on extended credit.

By the spring of 1970, against all odds, it seemed as if George and the others were going to be successful with their project. Timothy had got the Communications Centre off the ground and it was developing a considerable reputation as a media-training institution in Asia. Through an American friend George had met a wealthy American financier, Herman Kingsley, who had raised the necessary two hundred million dollars to finance the first of the various projects, beginning with the Philippines, and then going on to other similar projects in Asia.

All conditions had been agreed and preliminary documents signed with the highest authorities in the Philippines, and Herman Kingsley flew to the Philippines with George's brother, Bill, as guests of President Marcos, to sign the final agreement with him. But it also required the signatures of two other leading members of his Cabinet, and as he was in the last months of his presidency and obstructed by a suspicious opposition, the President was unable to persuade them to sign. The money was on deposit in a leading American bank, with holding costs of US$30,000 a day, so after fourteen days' delay and a loss of US$420,000, Herman Kingsley cancelled the arrangement and returned to the United States.

It was a shattering blow to everybody concerned, for so many bills had been postponed for the past almost three years, in the expectation of being able to pay once the first contract was signed, that we were all in very serious circumstances. George came back to Hong Kong physically, mentally and spiritually exhausted. When he went to see government agencies, such as the income tax authorities, to seek further consideration, they were unsympathetic and threatened that if he did not pay what was owed immediately he would be put in prison and all our household goods confiscated and sold. Having been three years away from media reporting of Chinese and Asian affairs, George was finding it difficult to get back into the competitive field of journalism to earn money. The authorities then decided to garnishee (or, arbitrarily requisition) my salary at source for the next six months in order to reduce our tax liability, leaving us with no income at all to pay for anything.

What we would have done with no money, no jobs (or, in my case, a job but no pay) and no home, in Hong Kong, I could not imagine. But two close friends, Seamus and Gerry Rainbird, stepped in when they heard of our predicament, and out of their own resources paid our income tax debt, keeping George out of prison. They also took our children into their own home when we had to vacate our flat. George and I had only our old car in which to live until another two friends gave us a tiny room in their flat in the poorer part of Hong Kong. Eventually, George got work with the local radio and television networks and started writing again.

But, bad as things were in the material realm, the most serious consequence of the whole 'world-changing communications enterprise' was the destruction of our spiritual life. Everyone involved had been so confident that God had willed and designed the whole project—and its incredible development to the very point of success, awaiting only President Marcos' signature, seemed to confirm divine approval—that its public collapse into humiliating failure left several of the leading participants bewildered and bitter against God. The interpersonal relationships which had existed between families and friends deteriorated and snapped, adding to the resentments towards each other and God.

George dropped all his preaching and teaching, and we stopped attending church services. We kept up our daily family devotions in the morning, as part of our parental responsibilities towards the upbringing of our children; but where before the spiritual had given meaning and purpose and force to our lives it now played no part at all—except that I was unable to rid myself of the conviction that God was refusing to let me go altogether.

George, typically in character, was more extreme in his reaction. His conviction was that his personal commitment to God to order all circumstances of life had been shown to be worthless in a humiliatingly public way, not only in having prayers go unanswered but leaving us bereft of even the least support for our family. The righteous had been forsaken and the children left without bread. But we were both rebellious at the way we had apparently been betrayed by the God we had trusted.

Ironically, within a few months President Marcos declared martial law, took over dictatorial power in the Philippines and sent a representative to Hong Kong to renew the discussions with George regarding the financing of the satellite network and other projects they had discussed. George had had enough, however, and he refused to be further involved.

Meanwhile, Timothy Yu had been incredibly successful with his Communications Centre, and it was now established as part of the Chinese University with full government recognition, turning out highly skilled graduates in all forms of media. It had even been classed by the international UNESCO as 'the second most important communications development in the world' of the time. The 'Christian Communications Revolution' envisaged by George and his friends had not been such a pipe dream after all; it had only failed (to change the metaphor) at the last hurdle. But it also added a bitter taste to the disappointment.

Gradually George picked up writing and broadcasting work again, and then the Hong Kong Government suddenly asked him if he would write a definitive book about the drug problem in Hong Kong. With the expansion of the war in Vietnam, and the United States committing more and more troops, drug trafficking in Asia had exploded into a monumental crisis. The war was a perfect cover for the growth and distribution of opium and its derivatives as the American soldiers picked it up at giveaway prices, the CIA and the Asian forces organised its operations, and the soldiers carried it as couriers across Asia and into the United States when they went on leave. American soldiers pouring off ships and aircraft for 'rest and recreation' in Asian cities brought with them their leave pay in 90% heroin powder instead of cash, and then traded it for large profits in the bars and nightclubs. The Chinese secret societies fastened onto this unexpected distribution bonus, and soon heroin packets were being sold at school playgrounds as commonly as sweets and peanuts—and almost as cheaply.

It was this situation which caused official concern at high government level in Hong Kong and led them to approach George, who was well-known for his writing and broadcasting about the drug problem. They offered him every co-operation in his investigations when he expressed his scepticism about the supposed willingness of the officials to talk. But when firm assurances were given him at the highest level, he finally agreed to write the book.

We had already been having quite a number of teenagers coming to the house to talk with George about drug abuse in the schools, and also to talk about the occult in which many of them were dabbling too. Soon after our arrival in Hong Kong George had been asked to address youth groups because of his experiences in Tibet, and to show his films, and in the discussions afterwards many of the teenagers asked if they could talk with him privately at home. These numbers now increased as George actively sought specific information to include in his book.

We had long discussions about what to do with our children when these teenagers came to talk, for many of them liked to boast about the quantity of drugs they could take 'without becoming addicted', how they could process different drugs in the school laboratories without the teachers knowing, the wonderful 'highs' they could have which gave them extraordinary insights, their thrilling encounters with criminal drug-peddlers, their deceptions of parents and teachers and police—all usually accompanied by the use of deliberately shocking foul language. At the time (1971) our children's ages were: Lorne twelve, Sean ten, and Myrrh eight. We decided that, since they were exposed to some, if not all, of these influences at school anyway, it would be beneficial if they were allowed to stay up at home and hear what we had to say in reply to their schoolmates in our own home.

It was very difficult at times, for many of the teenagers were children of friends and acquaintances, who did not know that their children were on drugs. So, in their homes, or at cocktail parties, or on official occasions, we would hear a father or mother inveighing against the existing modern situation of ungrateful children, affluent teenagers, generation gaps, indulgent teachers—and thanking God that their children were not like that!

The lid finally blew off the increasingly explosive situation, as far as European youth were concerned, with the death of one of them, Barry Laubach, in January, 1972. Barry was the teenage only son of a well-to-do American business family, active members of the Baptist Church. He was an intelligent, popular student, polite and well-liked by adults, and an admired school captain. He had been with his parents early in the evening of New Year's Eve, and then they went off to some celebration, leaving him at home.

Next morning, when they went to Barry's room to see what was keeping him in bed so late, they found him dead of an overdose of drugs. On investigation, he was found to be one of a group of top students at the American International School who not only took a variety of drugs, but also trafficked in them to others. It was also discovered just how widespread was the abuse of drugs in the other schools as shocked and frightened children, in the aftermath of Barry's death and the subsequent exposures, confessed to their parents and authorities what was happening. Some of the children felt so guilty about Barry's death that they arranged with occult-practising friends to conduct a special seance in order to make contact with Barry's departed spirit, so that they could exchange messages. One of the girls in the group had two familiar spirits that she contacted regularly for requests by her friends, from homework questions to finding their lost pets.

Parents were outraged, the news media went in full cry after the Government, crisis meetings were held at all levels demanding that something be done immediately about 'the drug problem'. George, who knew what was really involved at criminal, political and financial level, was sceptical about anything other than temporary cosmetic action being taken. With all the supposed authorisation he was promised by top officials he was having the greatest difficulties in getting government officials to meet and talk with him, other than to repeat the usual platitudes.

Until this time I had viewed the discussions in the home as George's responsibility, although I sat in on them and took part where I had a contribution. But with Barry's death, and the shocked reaction of his friends, I became more personally involved with the whole drug problem. Barry's death was shocking at one level, but so was the knowledge that one of the living thirteen-year-old girls had already injected so much heroin into her veins that she had none left to take the needle—and she was now injecting under her tongue. She was the same age as Lorne.

Over the next several months I did personal investigations into the extent of the drug problem in the hospital, and among my patients. I was astonished to learn from my Chinese medical colleagues, who had become so accustomed to the circumstances that they were no longer shocked at official disinterest, that drug taking and drug trafficking in one form or another was an essential part of everyday Hong Kong life. It was a priority activity of the feared Chinese 'Triads'; it generated astronomical profits for them so that they could pay for informers everywhere at all levels of government—and certainly in the hospitals, too.

It was officially estimated that there were at least 300,000 full Triad members in Hong Kong—compared with only 2,000 members of the Cosa Nostra (Mafia) in the United States. There were more than fifty separate Triad organisations, and within one of the largest, the '14K', there were supposed to be at least 50 sub-groups. The criminal secret societies held Hong Kong in a gigantic web of malevolent exploitation and death. What chance had the children against such an enemy, that even governments feared? I did not know it at the time, but I was about to be drawn into that evil, subterranean world of crime, extortion and exploitation through a new development in my medical experience.

In 1972 President Richard Nixon of the United States went to China on a historic visit, taking with him an unprecedented entourage of media and medical personnel. When James Reston of the *New York Times* had to have a surgical operation in Peking, and was treated successfully by Chinese electroacupuncture, it evoked great interest in the media and medical circles and there were scores of articles about the remarkable uses of electroacupuncture in all kinds of illnesses and operations in China.

A neurosurgeon colleague of mine, Dr H. L. Wen, a

consultant at the Tung Wah Hospital, decided to visit China to study electroacupuncture for use as an anaesthetic in his brain operations at the Tung Wah Hospital.

I had known about acupuncture for several years. While we were in London, George's colleague, Guy Wint, had asked me to see Dr Felix Mann, one of the leading Western doctors trained in acupuncture in China, with a view to having Guy treated by him for pain following a cerebral haemorrhage. I had met Felix Mann several times and had been very impressed by his attitude and results, especially after Guy had been treated successfully by him in modifying his symptoms. At that time George had been helping Guy to edit a book, *Handbook on Asia*, and they had included an essay on the subject of 'Acupuncture'. In Hong Kong, we had become friendly with a leading Chinese doctor, L. K. Ding, and he had been instrumental in obtaining official government approval to introduce the three-thousand-year-old Chinese traditional medical practices, such as acupuncture by skilled specialists, into Hong Kong. I had often sent patients for acupuncture treatment, and had it used successfully on George and myself on occasions.

*Electro*acupuncture, however, was a fairly recent innovation. The Chinese Communist authorities only introduced electrical stimulation about 1960 when they began to do major operations requiring lengthy analgesia, and in order not to have several people standing at the operating table for several hours, twirling acupuncture needles every few minutes. The electrical stimulator which they attached to the acupuncture needles by leads provided a regular electrical pulse which removed the need for individuals to tap or twirl the needles. It was this process which had so startled and excited the media and medical personnel accompanying President Nixon, as they watched wide-awake patients talking to surgeons, or sipping liquids, while undergoing major surgery.

Dr Wen returned just as excited and enthusiastic as the Western doctors. One of the still puzzling features of electroacupuncture in China, however, even after half a million operations had been done using this method, was why ten per cent of those 'needled' did not respond with analgesia to the same needling as the others. For this reason everybody was given a preliminary needling, in order to make certain that they were responsive before any operation.

Dr Wen showed me, and two other doctors in the Tung Wah Hospital, how to insert the needles to effect the desired response. One of the Chinese doctors, Dr Cheung, was a surgeon whom I had trained for his Fellowship in surgery, and the other was a physician in charge of the medical wards. Within a few weeks we were getting some startling side-effects to the needling which he did not expect, and which he had not heard about during his visit to China.

Patients who were in the hospital for operations spontaneously offered the information that, since the needling began, they had reduced the number of cigarettes they smoked; or they had reduced or stopped their opium, morphine or heroin intake; or they had lost their desire for alcohol; or their chronic asthma had eased considerably. At first we paid little attention, for they seemed unrelated to their conditions, but soon Dr Wen was asking if there could be any connection between the electroacupuncture needling and the unusual unsolicited responses we were being given by the patients.

We decided to do a series of controls in both the surgical and medical wards, taking carefully detailed case histories from the patients concerned regarding their smoking, snorting, injecting drug habits, their alcohol drinking, their records of treatment for asthma, chronic pain and other conditions, as well as the symptoms for whatever operation they were undergoing. Taking opium or heroin in Hong Kong was not a crime, and there was no social stigma attached to the practice, but trafficking was a crime. The older Chinese still mostly used opium, but the younger addicts nearly all used heroin. The two most popular brands were 'No. 3', a combination of about forty per cent heroin and sixty per cent barbitone; and 'No. 4', over ninety per cent pure heroin. It was the 'No. 3' packet which sold on the streets for less than the price of a packet of cigarettes. The daily dose of an average addict was three packets of 'No. 3'.

We selected forty patients for the first study—thirty opium and ten heroin addicts—whose ages ranged from seventeen to seventy-nine years, and where the duration of addiction ranged from three to fifty-eight years. We decided to change the standard acupuncture 'points' for total body analgesia to inserting into each ear 'lung point' only, and attaching the leads to the standard '6.26' Chinese pulse generator. About ten to fifteen minutes after stimulation began their eyes and nose became dry; the aching, shivering and abdominal pain decreased; breathing became regular, and they felt warm and relaxed. Often, they fell asleep after thirty or forty minutes of treatment, and woke feeling refreshed and hungry, communicative and alert. By the tenth day of repeated treatments they claimed they had lost their craving as well as all their drug withdrawal symptoms.

The four doctors conducting the experimental treatments all had their own surgical and medical responsibilities, and so all of these researches into the effects of electroacupuncture on drugs had to be conducted in our own 'spare time'. It was difficult for us to do regular urine tests, but out of twenty-two which we tested all were negative, except for two who were receiving analgesics or sedatives for other conditions. It was obvious to us that we were being confronted by an unknown and exciting new development in drug treatment, but one with too few clues on which to build an acceptable hypothesis. In my discussions with my Chinese colleague, Dr L. K. Ding, who had a deep knowledge of Chinese traditional medicines, I had learned that in three thousand years of orthodox acupuncture with needles but no electrical stimulator attached, there was no recorded instance of curing drug addiction in China. It had only a mild beneficial effect as a muscle relaxant. Therefore, it seemed to me, our remarkable responses had to be something to do with the electrical stimulation. But Dr Wen was convinced that the secret lay in the acupuncture system, and he concentrated his free-time efforts in this area.

During the next few months over one hundred Chinese addicts were treated in this way, without any psychotherapy or counselling whatever, and with the minimum of hospital care because doctors and surgeons and nurses all had their own lists of patients and ward duties to attend to, and the drug addicts were a begrudged extra burden for the greatly overworked staff.

At that time the famous neurosurgeon, Dr Irving Cooper of St Barnabas Hospital in New York, visited Hong Kong to deliver a series of lectures about his cryogenic surgical techniques. Dr Cooper had developed the first successful treatment of Parkinson's disease, and was known world-wide as 'the father of cryogenic surgery' (the technique of destroying certain tiny areas of brain cells by freezing them with the tip of a probe inserted into the brain). We met him socially as well, and in the course of one conversation he told me that his new interest was the use of electrical stimulation by implanted electrodes in the brain for the treatment of chronic epilepsy and spasticity. We talked at length about the use of electrical stimulation, and I learned from him that there were a number of scientists and surgeons very interested in its possibilities as a whole new form of treatment which in time would replace chemotherapy.

I not only knew nothing about electrical stimulation in medicine, I knew nothing about electronics. I could change a fuse, and that was about all. But the dramatic nature of what I was seeing happening with the drug addict patients daily—especially when taken in the context of our personal family involvement with young drug addict friends, and the complexities of the drug problem internationally—and the immense potential if a scientifically accredited system of treatment of addiction could be devised, fascinated me. I began reading widely whatever I could find about electrical stimulation in medicine and surgery. I also began reading George's notes on the drug problem, which he had accumulated over the past several years.[3]

A cure for addiction! It was a mind-shattering possibility, and it dominated my thinking in a way that nothing had done since I first thought about doing surgery. I knew from George's notes that it was considered by leading international authorities as 'the world's worst social evil', and accepted as being 'incurable'. Yet I was watching it being cured before me every day. In the world's worst 'drug city', with drug addicts using the world's purest heroin, I was seeing them coming off opiates and alcohol and cigarettes, in a matter of weeks at the most.

I was consumed with the scope and potential of the possibilities; I could not get enough literature on the subject. George's satellite vision of the past few years was dwarfed before the immensity of this challenge. But, because of the collapse of our spiritual faith, neither of us were now concerned about a world-encompassing means of effectively communicating the Christian gospel. We were both aware of the irony and the tragedy, but too battered by the recent disappointments to do anything about it. We had enough to do dealing with the immediate political and medical problems.

Meanwhile, the Hong Kong Government put a sudden stop to all speculation on the subject. Dr Wen had given a lecture to a packed lecture hall of doctors, and was afterwards told by the Director of Health not to do so again on peril of official disciplinary action. Also, no statements were to be made to the media, who had begun to take an

---

[3] For the professional medical account of my investigations see my book, *Hooked? NET: The New Approach to Drug Cure* (London, UK and Boston, USA: Faber & Faber, 1986; Stuttgart, Germany: Klett-Cotta, 1988); 4th edition to be published under the title *The Addicted: The Revolutionary NeuroElectric Therapy* (Milton Keynes, UK: Nelson Word, 1994).

interest in early reports of our findings. George had written a two-part account of our investigations for the *South China Morning Post*, and had sent a shortened version to the *Observer* in London.

I was in a real quandary. I was now convinced beyond any shadow of doubt that we had stumbled serendipitously upon a major medical and scientific discovery of potentially immense benefit to the world, yet here I was faced with bureaucratic blindness and stubbornness, and parochial prejudice, combining to suppress it. However, there seemed to be little I could do about this. George could take on the bureaucracy yet again, but he would have to have ongoing research as backup material to use in publicity. And, as both Dr Wen and myself were surgeons employed by a government-funded institution, neither of us professional researchers, there was no way in which we could proceed with investigation of our theories in Hong Kong. But George and a journalist friend began to make a filmed record of some aspects of the treatment for the future.

For the first time in my life I began to give serious thought to the possibility of giving up surgery. It had never crossed my mind, except for the period when the children were younger, and then I only saw it as temporary. Now I knew that if this discovery was as important as I was concluding, and if I followed my increasing interest in the subject, then it might mean stopping my surgery.

It could all have ended there if (now Sir) Yehudi Menuhin, the world-famous violinist, and his pianist sister, Hephzibah, had not visited Hong Kong. They were performing at the First Hong Kong International Music Festival, and George had invited them to the house to visit us between performances. He had known Hephzibah and her sociologist husband, Richard Hauser, for many years and had shared some of their social work in London. When Yehudi and Hephzibah came to visit us, and I told them about our recent discovery about a possible cure for drug addiction, they were enthralled and wanted to see the process. I took them to the Tung Wah Hospital, and they were so impressed they insisted that I must pursue the research at whatever personal cost, and they would help me.

Then, as George had suspected, the Hong Kong Government decided they could not proceed with the publication of the definitive book about the drug problem after all. Despite their assurances regarding his having every official co-operation, leading officials of all departments stalled on making appointments, or cancelled them, or evaded his relevant questions, or forgot to send promised documents. George knew that many of them were either directly, or indirectly through their children, involved with police who were the official paymasters of bribes for the Chinese Triads.

Eventually, George prepared a ten-thousand-word précis of the material he had gathered, sent it to the Government Information Service officials who were monitoring the drug book for publication, and told them that unless he received information to the contrary this was the substance of the book he would write. This action—and the return to Hong Kong of (now Sir) Jack Cater, a top official and a good friend of George's—brought an immediate response from the government: instructions not to proceed with the project. They could not be officially associated with such a damning indictment. George's arrangement in terminating the contract was that he would not use his privileged information for a year—unless someone in the Government made uninformed or tendentious statements about the drug problem which would reflect on his own professional reputation.

With the earlier official approval, however, George had been able to have an unprecedented insight into the whole drug scene in Hong Kong. Also, through his official contacts and status, he met with visiting drug treatment experts from other countries who came to Hong Kong to see what was being done. From all this experience we deduced that, shorn of the superficial verbiage, there was little effective treatment being provided anywhere. When leading experts came from Britain or America or Australia to investigate the optimistic claims of the Hong Kong Government's alternative-to-prison treatment process, they were not unduly impressed. They would have been even less impressed had they known that the long-term recidivism, or relapse, rate was ninety per cent.

Being Christians ourselves, we were particularly interested in Christian treatment programmes for drug addicts in Hong Kong and elsewhere. But when we submitted them to the same objective scrutiny as all other treatments they were no better, and often worse, than others.

A US Government study by the National Institute on Drug Abuse of the American Christian drug treatment used by Teen Challenge, over a period of seven years, showed that their statistics of success were little better than other similar programmes. An interesting supplementary analysis of the study was that some thirty per cent of the unsuccessful addicts were Christians, some sixteen per cent of whom had been 'baptised by the Holy Spirit' with equal lack of success.

There were a number of these programmes in Hong Kong, the one run by a young woman becoming most favoured by media interest (the first producer to film her work being George's colleague, Chris Menges—against George and Adrian's advice, let it be said). She claimed that she could cure all drug addictions by means of 'speaking in tongues', a wholly unscriptural concept apart from anything else, as neither Jesus nor any of His disciples ever used 'speaking in tongues' as a means of cure. Nor were we impressed by the Christian group associated with the drug work (although the leaders had come to Hong Kong en route to China because they were influenced by George's book, *God's Fool!*), as George and I were having to sort out the members' problems of sex, marriage, and other spiritual misdemeanours—despite the supposed potency of speaking in tongues.'[4]

Another work, which impressed us much more, was carried out by a Chinese pastor, John Paul Chen. It was known as 'Operation Dawn', and was located on a remote island near to the mainland of China. Pastor Chen took in most of the rejects of all other treatment centres, provided a strict regime of self-help and individual responsibility in addition to fundamental spiritual principles, and then put the inmates back into their normal environments with other Christians providing ongoing spiritual support.

On one occasion I went with George on a visit to Pastor Chen's treatment centre—and will never forget the experience! We went by car up the Kowloon peninsula to the New Territories' waterfront village of Saikung. There Pastor Chen had a small boat with an outboard motor to take us to the island. The two bench seats in the centre only held two people each, and the boatman was an ex-addict called Paul, who sat operating the rudder on the gunwale next to the motor.

It was a glorious, calm day and the small boat put-putted its way for an hour or so across the glassy China Sea to the distant small island. We spent an interesting time talking with the inmates and counsellors, then in late afternoon prepared to return to Hong Kong.

The sun had stopped shining, but the sea around the island was still calm as we waved goodbye. However, when we reached the open sea beyond the inlet the rain started, the wind suddenly increased, and the boat began slapping against the foam-topped waves sweeping towards us.

At first I didn't bother, as I loved the sea and anything to do with boats, and was more concerned about George who got sea-sick when the sea was rough. But when the skies darkened into one of the region's notorious sudden

---

[4] For full details of our conclusions regarding the reasons for success and failure in Christian treatment of drug addictions see *The Paradise Factor*, by George and Meg Patterson (Milton Keynes: Nelson Word, 1994).

storms, and the small boat had to climb huge waves towering above us like skyscrapers, I was really worried.

What was remarkable was the aplomb of Pastor Chen and Paul the boatman. Paul continued to sit on the gunwale, as he had done on the outward trip, calmly guiding the boat down the black troughs of the waves and then up the sheer slopes of the far sides, while Pastor Chen baled out the drenching water with a tin can. When the boat reached the foaming peaks of the monster waves it hung there, poised, with its propeller spinning out of the water, until it got sufficient purchase to proceed down the other side.

I thought we would never survive the endless battering, and the accompanying terrifying thunder-and-lightning storm, but eventually we edged out of the maelstrom into the calm waters of Saikung and we were safe. Pastor Chen and Paul were unperturbed and said it was quite a regular happening. And George had no sea-sickness!

A few months after giving George their assurances that there would be no official attempts to whitewash the drug situation in Hong Kong, a government spokesman began to make public statements which directly countered what George had uncovered. Even the news media were outraged at the bland misinformation, and they challenged the spokesman to provide evidence of his officially approved claims. So George started writing and broadcasting about specific acts of corruption which he had uncovered in the various departments during his investigations—especially the Police, Anti-Triads and Customs. All hell broke loose.

Many of the officials were aware that George knew of the involvement of their own children with drugs; and of the blackmail of the parents by the police, or by the Triads. The children, who were terrified of exposure, had told us in their conversations with us of the tactics of the police in 'framing' them for either possession or trafficking in order to get a hold over them.

We had warned our own children about this practice, and told them never to stop to speak to strangers in the street without a witness, and to be especially careful of policemen in uniform. This was extremely difficult for them as they either forgot, or were in situations where they found it embarrassing or even impossible to comply. George also began to receive veiled—and sometimes not-so-veiled—threats because of his high-profile public campaign against the drug trafficking and corruption.

So, when Yehudi and Hephzibah wrote to us after their return to London to say that they had spoken with various interested people about our drug discovery and that we should seriously consider coming to Britain to pursue research there, we began to make plans to do so. Hephzibah said that she and Richard would take in the children, and see to their schooling, while we wound up our affairs in Hong Kong.

Then an American family who lived in France visited us at the suggestion of mutual friends. They had a son of Sean's age—ten years old—and as they became close friends the parents proposed that we send Sean back to France with them to study with their son for a year. We had decided never to break up the family, because of the havoc we had seen in other families when they sent their children away for education and other reasons, but since they were now under real threat in Hong Kong we considered that changed matters, and we let him go. In the event, Sean—who knew no French when he left Hong Kong—spent an unforgettable year in France where he attended a French school. His teacher spoke no English, but Sean even learned to speak German as well as French, and finished at the top of his class.

We quickly sold off the few possessions we had accumulated and arranged to return to Britain after almost ten years in Hong Kong. When all our fares were paid it left us with no money once again. This time there was a significant difference, however. Our decisions had all been made without prayer and discussions with God, and the reason for our going was because of a vision of mine and not of George.

We did not slip away quietly, although that was how we planned it. We had arranged to spend our last night in Hong Kong with our good friends, (now Sir and Lady) Roger and Margaret Lobo. When we arrived Margaret and I chatted inside, while Roger and George moved out to the verandah. Before we got on to family conversation Roger wanted to have a serious political talk with George.

Some time before, George had told Roger, in Roger's capacity as senior Legislative Councillor, of the critical aspects of the drug problem in Hong Kong. He had told him—without naming names—of the influence at the highest level of the government of the Chinese Triads, of how they could even manipulate the Governor's decisions. Roger now wanted to know if George would reveal the identity of such a highly placed official, and also free him from the obligations of confidentiality because he wanted to inform the Governor. It seemed that at the weekly meeting of the Governor's five advisers, of whom Roger was now one, the Governor had informed them that there was a high-level agent of the Triads among his advisers and he was determined to expose him. Roger wanted to give the Governor the name uncovered by George, with his permission. George agreed, and told him the name of someone never suspected by Roger and well-known to him.

The next day, before we left for the airport, Jack Cater telephoned George to ask for more details, and George provided them. Several months later, the Governor set up a judicial tribunal, with a respected judge from London, to investigate corruption in government, out of which was formed an Independent Commission against Corruption, headed by Jack Cater. This was the start of a sweeping clean-out of corrupt officials at the highest government levels. We left Hong Kong safely.

- 6 -
My New Medical Career in London

We arrived back in London in July, 1973. Hephzibah and Richard put up beds for us and the children; and, with Yehudi, helped me begin my new professional venture. George was on call right away for media interviews regarding drug trafficking in south-east Asia, and the police corruption in Hong Kong, which had exploded into the international news. Hephzibah had got the children into Pimlico Comprehensive School, which helped us with the educational problem.

But as I met with various people in medical and scientific circles it became quickly apparent that, while there was considerable interest in the new phenomenon of China's electroacupuncture, there was little money available for experimentation. What money was available was going to recognised orthodox researchers, and certainly not to me as an unknown surgeon.

Another apparently insuperable obstacle in Britain was the arrangement in the National Health Service whereby psychiatrists alone were given the responsibility to be consultants in the drug and alcohol addiction fields. Also, any money available went to the few specialists already in the field, with none available for me as a surgeon, despite my experience.

In desperation I applied, successfully, for a post as a surgeon in the Prison Service, where it was implied that I could devote some of my time to researching the possibilities of electroacupuncture for drug addiction. But a professional friend warned me to be sure to get the promise in writing, for it was his conviction that it was only a ruse to get me in as a surgeon and then refuse me permission— regretfully, of course—to do research. I could not obtain the assurance in writing, so I resigned the offered post four days before I was due to start work.

Meanwhile, Yehudi had arranged for me to meet friends of his who could help with other aspects of my research. I had decided that the regular Chinese acupuncture needles were not necessary for what I wanted to do, and that I needed a tension ear-clip with a minute, built-in needle which would be more tolerable for Europeans when inserted in the sensitive ear concha. Yehudi introduced me to Andrew Grima, the jeweller to the Queen, and he made my first ear-clip without charge—of white gold.

Then through Yehudi and Andrew Grima I was introduced to David Shackman, an electronics engineer, who had a company producing audio-visual equipment. He agreed to help me, without payment, to construct an electrical stimulator which would include my own theories regarding requisite electrical frequencies and wave-forms for the treatment of drug addictions.

And so I began another new study, in bioelectronics. There was some literature available in the West on the subject, but it was nothing compared with the amount compiled in East European countries. I was fascinated and excited by the potential that was emerging from the various experiments.

From what I had learned, I had to work out by trial and error on myself the actions, reactions and interactions of frequencies and wave-forms, and then communicate my findings back to Geoffrey Bennett, the manager of Shackmans, to get the kind of physical response I needed to elicit from an electrical stimulus. I was able to get theoretical advice from professional colleagues in Northwick Park Science Laboratories in North London, and from the

Wolfson Science Laboratories of the Strathclyde University in Scotland. Yehudi and Hephzibah rounded up friends who were prepared to help as guinea pigs, or who had acquaintances who were addicted to some form of chemical, and who were happy to try anything that might help. But it was laborious, time-consuming work—and unpaid.

Hephzibah's daughter was coming home and this meant we had to find a place of our own in which to live. The only income we had was George's diminishing freelance journalism earnings. Because I was out researching most of the day he had to attend to the children and household duties, and it did not leave much time for writing.

He went to see the Bank of Scotland manager, where we had kept an account for many years, to see if the bank could help. Considering our totally penniless, and unsecured, circumstances, they were amazingly helpful; offering to let us have £10,000—but on condition that both of us took up regular jobs in our professions, particularly myself as a surgeon. But I could not find an appointment that would permit me time or opportunity to research the drug treatment at the same time as doing surgery, so we turned down the bank's generous offer and plodded on. We were now reduced to living in cheap lodgings in Victoria, eating with Hephzibah and Richard, and George was on Social Security—queuing with new immigrants, and being aggressively questioned by suspicious civil servants.

One day when I returned home from visiting one of the hospitals I found that George had fixed an appointment for us to look at a flat and consulting room—in, of all places, Harley Street, the mecca of all medical practitioners. I had no ambition to live or practise in Harley Street. Even to consider it in our present impecunious circumstances was the most ridiculous of all the many harebrained schemes that George had dreamed up in our memorable lives. However, George had already made the appointment to visit the premises the next morning, and, after much persuasion, I agreed to go with him.

That evening we were at dinner with wealthy friends, Dick and Pamela Knight, who some years before had developed a deep interest in Tibet, and in helping the Tibetan people, through George's persuasion. They had unofficially adopted the son and daughter of Surkhang Shapay, our Tibetan Cabinet Minister friend, and had sent them to the best schools in England for an education.

When, during dinner conversation, I told them what George was suggesting for the next day, they were as astounded as I was. They, too, had had some experience of George's escapades in the past, and always enjoyed the *frisson* of excitement that these generated. When George argued that my only hope was to impress the medical establishment—and in order to do that I needed status and not just statistics—Pamela thought he was only being provocative and dropped the subject. But Dick continued to discuss it with George between themselves, while Pamela and I discussed the children and their education. Dick and Pamela had offered to pay for our children's education at the best public schools in Britain, and we had even taken them to see Westminster School next to the Houses of Parliament, where the boys' names had been registered, to decide for themselves. But they had chosen to stay on in Pimlico Comprehensive, which they liked. It was the usual quiet, pleasant evening.

Next morning George and I went to see the flat in Harley Street, and I felt like I had on that occasion in Edinburgh during our honeymoon when we went into the fashion dress salon. George had the same sort of look about him, the same too-innocent smile when he looked at me. It was a small, but delightfully furnished flat on the second floor at the north, or Regent's Park, end of Harley Street. As we walked from room to room George would solemnly consult me about the suitability of the kitchen equipment, or the accessibility of the consulting rooms which were at the far end of the hall.

I had noticed right away that, despite its many attractive features, it was much too small for our requirements as a family, so I was certain that whatever George was up to it could not end up in our doing anything about the flat. My earlier trepidation had eased, therefore, and I was able to discuss fairly reasonably some of the points he raised, knowing that I was going to turn it down.

That was when I heard George ask the landlord if he would have any objection to our bringing our three children—two boys and a girl, aged thirteen, eleven and nine—to live in the flat with us! The landlord looked surprised, as well he might, for it was only a one-bedroom flat, and he replied that he thought it was much too small. But, he went on to suggest, he had some unoccupied rooms in the basement which could be renovated, but what would we do in the meantime? George smoothly suggested that he could bring in a fold-down couch for the children until the rooms were ready—if we could agree terms. 'But I think we should go and talk it over,' George said to the landlord, looking questioningly at me. I could only nod speechlessly. What was there to talk over? But at least it offered a means of escape from this impossible situation.

'I would like to have your decision as soon as possible,' the landlord said firmly. 'I have another client coming after lunch, and I would like to know by then what you decide.'

'No problem,' George agreed amicably. 'We'll just go and have a chat over a cup of coffee, and then phone you about our decision.'

I started on George just as soon as the outside door shut behind us, but he was maddeningly enigmatic and provocative. To all my objections he would say, 'Where is you faith?' or, 'The Lord will provide' or, 'With an address like that you'll conquer the medical world—they won't ask you for proof, they'll ask for your card.'

Only when he had ordered coffees did he become serious—if that is the word in such circumstances.

'All right,' he said at last. 'Do you like the place or not?'
When I would have argued he refused, and repeated the
question.

'Of course I like the place,' I conceded in exasperation,
'but that's not the point. It costs three thousand pounds a
year just to rent, and then we have to find the money to eat.
And that doesn't include the extra money to be paid for the
rooms for the children.'

'I have every confidence in your ability–' George began
with mock seriousness, then dissolved into laughter. 'Sorry
about that,' he continued, 'but, like Scaramouche, I was
"born with a gift of laughter and a sense that the world is
mad". But I will be serious now. Look, dear, from my
cynical experience it is my opinion that you are not going to
make it with your medical discovery as you are. Unlike me,
you are not equipped to take people by the scruff of their
stubborn necks and shake them until their tiny shrivelled
brains rattle in their bone-thick heads. You are too gentle,
too polite, you play by the book rules—and the establishment know these better than you do, and is ready for you
before you even appear. You are not known in the centres
of power or status; your work has been done abroad, and has
been with the poor. You come back to this country with a
supposed cure for all addictions—a field notorious for its
specious claims, and dominated by the most prejudiced and
tendentious school of medical practitioners, the
psychiatrists. And, worst of all, the cure arises from
acupuncture, an oriental system loaded with gobbledegook.
I have watched you get the classic runaround for the past
few months. Now, before you answer my question about the
Harley Street flat seriously, I want you to take a deep
breath, pause and consider well, and answer another
question first: just how seriously do you take your
discovery? I know how you feel in a general way, but now
convince me as a sceptical journalist.' He sat back and
waited for an answer.

It was infuriating, but I knew he was right. I could

sense the patronising attitudes behind the polite interest of my medical colleagues in influential circles. And, realistically, I was no further forward to real acceptability than when I first arrived. But if I could not convince George who knew how real and deep was my interest, how was I going to convince others? I was in a Catch-22 situation in which I needed money for research which would validate my theories, and I needed valid research before I could get the money.

'I am so convinced that I am prepared to give up my surgery altogether,' I said slowly, thinking. 'I am convinced that this is a medical discovery of major importance which will compare with the great discoveries of the past. I am prepared to drop everything, do anything, see anybody, put up with all embarrassments, ignore every sneer, and concentrate on this alone for the next year at whatever cost.'

'Three years,' George interrupted. 'Maybe five. That's what it's going to take—if you're very lucky.'

'Whatever the time,' I emphasised. 'I *know* the answer is there. I just have to find it.'

'All right,' George said, leaning forward. 'That's enough for me. It was a fellow-scientist who said, if I remember correctly, that true genius does not consist in making great discoveries but in making the connection between a lot of small discoveries. You will need my help, so here's what I will do. God knows, you have helped me often enough in the past twenty years in just as far-fetched ventures as this. But you're going to have to take in some patients, if not for surgery then for treatment of addictions—unless someone comes up with money for your research. So, I will drop my journalism and other activities, to release you to give your whole time to this project. I'll be responsible for the shopping, cooking and other household activities, while you get on with the job. Now, tell me. Do you like the Harley Street flat, or not?'

'Of course I like it,' I said. 'Who wouldn't? But–'

'But me no buts,' George interrupted. 'As they say on

the TV before the commercials: "I'll be right back." ' He
rose from the table, and left me to my thoughts.

He returned a few minutes later and, sitting down, said:
'Well, it's yours. I've fixed it.'

When I said nothing, but just sat looking at him, he
grinned. 'When I talked with Dick last night,' he said in
explanation, 'he asked me if I was really serious about taking
the flat. I told him more or less what I have just told you:
that you'd never make it if you had to live in and work out of
Laburnum Grove or Acacia Avenue in the suburbs, and that
in my opinion you had to gamble everything on Harley
Street—and from there back up your claims with proof.
Dick asked me to give him a call when I had seen the place,
and gauged your reaction; and, if you wanted it, he and
Pamela would provide the rent out of the money they had
set aside for our children's education. So, you're on your
way, baby—and it's me for the hot stove in the kitchen.
Take it from there.'

It was a dream come true. As George had cynically
outlined, with the connections which Harley Street provided
in having well-known consultants of all kinds as neighbours,
in that one move I was able to begin a useful practice and
have substantive discussions with people and groups who
previously had never bothered to answer letters or return
telephone calls.

Our boys were enjoying Pimlico Comprehensive School
so much that we decided to leave them there, although it
involved a half-hour journey by underground train twice
daily. Myrrh was due to start there the next year. In the
meantime, she brought home her first boyfriend, also ten
years old. As she introduced him, George solemnly looked
him in the eye and declared, 'Young man, are your
intentions towards my daughter honourable?' It was many
years before Myrrh brought another boy home! George
never allowed life for us all to be too serious for too long.

I found a secretary with research experience, Louise
Mestel, and we prepared a formal submission to the Medical

Research Council for a grant. This took several weeks, having discussions with experts in a variety of disciplines in order to obtain their co-operation in the study, and it cost a lot of money in time lost when I could have been seeing patients. My life consisted now of crazy juggling with as few patients as possible, so that I had time for research, but as many as would pay for the research and necessary expenses.

Eventually, I received a reply rejecting my application, although the letter conceded the importance of my work to date. I knew some of the people at the Medical Research Council, and they told me privately later that the scientists among them were in favour of supporting my work, but that the psychiatrists were adamantly opposed, saying: 'She isn't a psychiatrist; she can't treat drug addicts.' In the official letter of rejection it said:

'You will by now have received the disappointing news that the Council does not feel able to support your project on acupuncture [*sic*] for the relief of craving in drug addicts. The Committee that considered it, however, asked me to tell you they very much hoped you would be able to do some work on the subject in your spare time. They felt that it was important that you should become familiar with the many problems that arise in dealing with drug addicts, and hoped that any job you decide to take may still leave you time to develop the contacts you have already made in the drug field . . .'

It would have been funny, if it had not been so tragic. From the reading of the letter one would assume that these psychiatrists were skilled experts in the field of drug addiction, instead of the most conspicuous failures—as their own statistics of treatment demonstrated. Yet this was to be the pattern of all my attempts to get financial help from official sources. The government's Department of Health and Social Security was worse than all the other bodies I approached, for we could not even get them to reply to letters most of the time. (George called them 'The Department of Stealth and Total Obscurity'.) When they did reply, after constant urging from us, they would suggest a meeting, compliment me on my work and interest, propose a membership of some already ineffective drug or alcohol committee, and regret their inability to do anything.

We decided to set up a charity of our own to see if we could raise money that way, and out of our own earnings we paid about a thousand pounds to lawyers to establish 'FREE! The National Institute for Healing of Addictions.' Yehudi and Hephzibah agreed to do a concert for us in the Royal Festival Hall; and Cliff Richard and Larry Norman, the rock music stars, also did a concert. Our advisory council included (now Sir) Yehudi Menuhin, Lord Harlech, H.R.H. Prince Peter of Greece and Denmark, General Sir Alec Bishop, the actor Sean Connery, and a number of other friends who had known our work in the past.

Then Eric Clapton was referred to me. I can use his name openly without any breach of medical ethics, because he has since been interviewed in the media and for books in which he discussed the treatment. At the time I did not know who he was, and George—and the children!—had to inform me. I was asked by Yehudi if I would meet Lord Harlech to discuss treating his daughter for heroin addiction. She was the girlfriend of Eric Clapton, and had become addicted through him. I was reluctant at that early stage of my research to take on such a public responsibility but Yehudi had been of such great help to me, and Lord Harlech was his close friend, that I agreed to do what I could to help.

Eric was, and still is, one of the world's great rock musicians, and many experts claim he is the world's greatest rock-blues guitarist. At one time apparently, when he and Jack Bruce and Ginger Baker were together in the famous rock group 'Cream', tens of thousands of placards declared 'Clapton is God' because of his inspired playing. But since then Eric had become a hopeless heroin addict, and for some years had been unable to play at all.

When Eric and Alice arrived for the first consultation,

they were tense and terrified at the thought of stopping their drugs; so, instead of seeing them in the consulting room, I put them in the sitting room with our children while I went to make a cup of tea. I returned to find Eric on the floor playing mock battles with Lorne and Sean and their model soldiers, and the tension all gone.

At first I tried treating Eric and Alice in his own home, but this was not convenient for several reasons and he agreed to come and live with us while I treated him. I managed to have Alice admitted to a small clinic nearby because she was in such a poor state of health, and was able to treat both at the same time.

Living in the flat with us meant that Eric had to sleep on the fold-down bed in the sitting room, the boys slept on a mattress on the floor, and Myrrh slept on the couch in my consulting room. The boys loved it. Eric bought a variety of records and they sat up for hours listening to the records while he taught them how to appreciate aspects of the great rock musicians' playing. We had warned them that if they stayed up late, they would still have to get up for school at the same time—which they did without complaint.

At this time I was using my first research model stimulator, a very cumbersome unit, and applying my version of acupuncture needles to the concha of the ear. This was a tedious and painful process as the ears became increasingly sensitive. At first neither Eric nor Alice believed that the treatment was really effective, until one night Eric complained that he had had a return of acute withdrawal symptoms all that day. Eric finally said he had not been feeling the current all day, and when I checked out the stimulator I found a wire had become disconnected. Once he was hooked up again there was an immediate and dramatic improvement—which convinced him that he was indeed responding to the stimulator. In this way, quite by accident, he became my first double-blind trial patient!

When we had guests we simply introduced Eric as a house guest, using his first name only, and most did not know who he was. But two of our guests who did know were Steve Turner and Norman Stone.

These were two friends whom George had met at an Arts Centre Group for Christians working in the arts and media. Steve was a writer, who had been an editor with leading rock music periodicals, and Norman was a film producer with the BBC. Unknown to us Steve and Eric had met previously, and both were startled to meet again in our home. However, it worked out very well, for Steve could keep quiet about Eric's presence with us for treatment, while at the same time providing interest and companionship for Eric while he was shut away. Later, Steve published a book, *Conversations with Eric Clapton*, from his talks with Eric during this period.

Another regular visitor to Eric while he was with us was his good friend Pete Townshend of 'The Who' rock group. As he saw Eric coming off his drug addiction Pete became very interested in the treatment and its possibilities for the many drug addicts in the rock music world. This was the beginning of a valued friendship as Pete involved himself closely with my research and, with the members of 'The Who', over the years held several concerts in support of my work.

Eric had brought a guitar with him, but I noticed that he never made any attempt to play; and once when I asked him to play something he refused gruffly. During one of his many conversations with George he said that one of the reasons he was on drugs was because he thought his musical creativity was disappearing. He argued that all the great jazz and blues musicians were on some form of stimulant, and this helped them with their creativity. George strongly opposed this, maintaining that the aesthetic sense was rooted in the spiritual, not in the chemical, and he asked Eric to demonstrate from his records where he played better under drugs. After doing so, Eric had to agree that the only performance that sounded better when he was on drugs was when he played his classic, 'Layla', with Derek and the

Dominoes. The rest he could have improved on without drugs.

During Eric's and Alice's treatment, which involved constant round-the-clock supervision to monitor the stimulator and their responses, George and I would just cat-nap when we could. I had dropped into bed exhausted one night when I was awakened by George talking. There was nothing unusual in this, except on this occasion he had switched on the light and asked Eric to come into the bedroom.

It appeared from what George said that he had been awakened from sleep by a voice, and naturally had thought it was Eric. But there had been no sound in the night, until a voice said, 'Pray with Eric.' His first reaction was to ignore it as subconscious prompting out of his spiritual past. But while he was still thinking it over—and noting that he was wide awake and clear-headed—the voice said again, 'Pray with Eric.' He knew then that he was on another collision course with God; that God was now forcing on him a decision that he had avoided for the past few years. And so he argued with God.

'Where were you when I needed you?' he demanded from God, and there was no reply. George knew why. The Scriptures made it clear that the clay does not say to the Potter: 'What doest Thou?' The clay has to be what the Potter makes it. George was not prepared for this, so he pointed out that he had stopped praying except for morning prayers with the children.

'Pray with Eric *now*,' the voice insisted. George was stubborn, and refused. He knew that what God wanted was his total unquestioning obedience as He had required it in the past, and the issue of praying with Eric in the middle of the night on a spoken command was only a test of his commitment. Obedience on this occasion would mean a return to the walk with God he had known in the past, before the satellite financing disaster.

'Pray with Eric NOW,' the voice commanded again.

George's resistance crumbled, and he agreed. That was when Eric had knocked on the door of our bedroom, saying, 'Are you awake, Meg?' This time, instead of calling out that I would be with him shortly, George had switched on the light, opened the door and invited Eric to come in.

When I awoke I knew nothing of what had transpired, of course; I only heard about it later from George. I sat up in bed as Eric entered, blinking in the light. George asked him to sit on the bed.

'Eric,' he said, 'I've been lying here for the past half-hour or so because I heard a voice telling me to pray with you, and I was reluctant to do so for several reasons. One of them was because I knew from what you said to me that you had had a bad experience with Christians in the United States some years ago, when they wanted to pray with you in public and you objected. But what you didn't know was that I also had a personal problem about God, part of which was that I did not want to be obedient any more to His commands. However, I had decided a few minutes ago that what God wanted God gets, and I was just going to come through and see you, when you knocked on the door. So, do I pray with you as God said?'

Eric's expression was a mixture of bewilderment and interest. 'Man,' he said, 'I have been lying there for the past half-hour myself, having a real black scene. So, go ahead.'

George prayed for himself, for Eric and for me in my work. When he had finished I asked Eric what he needed, but he said that he felt all right now. I got up to make some hot drinks for us, and left Eric and George talking quietly. When I returned with the drinks George was replying to a question by Eric as to what he should do next.

'There's you, there's your guitar, and there's God, Eric,' George said. 'All I can think of at this moment to add is two lines of a bit of rhyme:

"Lord, for tomorrow and its needs I do not pray,
  Give me, dear Lord, just give me, strength for today".'

The next day when I entered the sitting room Eric had his guitar, and was quietly playing some chords, eyes wet with unshed tears. He played no tune, but he made notes on a piece of paper.

Eric left after five weeks with us, for convalescence in the country for another few weeks. Then he went on to the United States to pick up his music career where it had been terminated so brutally by the heroin addiction. Three months later he was back on the world's stage, being applauded by the world's leading music critics as playing better than ever. One of the most acclaimed songs in his come-back record album, *Ocean Boulevard*, was a beautiful blues lullaby, entitled 'Give Me Strength', the words of which were:

'Dear Lord, give me strength to carry on,
Dear Lord, give me strength to carry on;
I've been out on the highway,
Lord, I've done so much wrong,
But please, give me strength to carry on.'

That became our own prayer once again, as God restored us spiritually following on that encounter. George looked for a church to attend, and we became part of a fellowship at Cholmley Evangelical Church in North London, where George once again began his preaching and teaching.

With the treatment of Eric Clapton a whole new phase of my work opened up. Pete Townshend had been so impressed by Eric's recovery that he and Eric talked with others needing treatment. This in turn brought in the rock music impresario, Robert Stigwood, who had launched his career as manager of the world-famous 'Cream' music group and now headed the wealthy Robert Stigwood Organisation. He and Ahmed Ertegun, of the American Atlantic Records music organisation, contributed generously to my research and sent rock musicians to me for treatment.

This produced an unexpected but exciting development, for many of these rock musicians were deeply interested and informed in electronics, which they used in their compositions. Their knowledge of the effects of electronics in music had interesting parallels with my own researches into the effects of frequencies in the mood alterations of the various addictions, and I was able to incorporate these findings into my medical device.

So, when the government departments or the medical and scientific establishments, who should have been helping me with the investigations, failed to do so, it was the much-maligned rock musicians who contributed at professional as well as financial levels.

With the publicity I was receiving through treating rock musicians I could have had more patients than I could handle, but one of the scandals of the drug addiction situation in Britain was the lack of adequate medical facilities for treating drug addicts. In fact, there were almost no facilities for *treating* drug addiction, but only a handful of places where drug addicts could go to be *maintained* legally on either their drug of addiction or by replacement drugs. If drug addicts got really bad, their doctor or psychiatrist might be able to get them into a mental institution. If they over-dosed they might be taken into the casualty or emergency wards of a hospital—although they were more often turned away—and sent out next morning when they had been pumped out. Addicts were the lepers of the twentieth century, it seemed.

I found this stigma at all levels of my work. Although addicts came from all classes of society, yet the general attitude, when we sought funds for research or for our charity to help, was that they deserved the consequences of their indulgence. Also, there was an unspoken implication that since nothing could really be done about addiction, it was not worth helping.

There were clinics or nursing homes for alcoholics, but these were solely for 'drying out'—although they claimed to be 'detoxification centres'. Doctors and psychiatrists were well aware of the failure of these places to detoxify—in the true sense of the term—and that most patients would be back on their alcohol shortly after they returned home. After all, doctors themselves headed the list of alcoholics in the professions. 'Physicians heal yourselves' could well be placed above the doors of every addiction unit.

Yet I could get no one to listen to me about the dramatic effects electrostimulation was having on just that detoxification condition. Certainly, there was more to curing addiction than simple detoxification, as I well knew, but since the experts were prepared to admit, albeit grudgingly, that 'simple detoxification is ineffective' and that this was still 'not understood', one would have thought that simple interest in the possibility might have appealed to their scientific minds.

I myself still did not have a satisfactory explanation for the phenomenon, but at least I was searching; while most of the experts I met tried to tell me that it was not possible to find a solution; or, worse still, without meeting me, or reading my material, they would appear in or write to the media, dismissing my work without any knowledge about it.

Despite these difficulties I was satisfied with the slow and steady improvement in my knowledge and techniques. When one patient fell asleep with the machine still on, and the needle-clip still in her ear, I discovered that I did not need needles at all. I could use surface electrodes attached to the leads and applied directly above the mastoid process behind the ear, and so I left all connection with acupuncture. This new technique also allowed me to apply the stimulator night and day instead of every few hours, with a dramatic improvement in its efficacy. Not only did it accelerate all the healing processes, it had an enormously beneficial effect on the usual insomnia of the addicts. Within a matter of days, instead of weeks, they were recovering the body's normal sleep pattern. It was only a short step from there to finding out the appropriate frequency to eliminate the horrifying nightmares experienced by the addicts as they came off their drugs.

Ever since I had treated Eric Clapton I had been bombarded by requests for interviews from the media in Britain and other countries, but I had firmly refused them all. I was not just afraid of the usual repercussions of discipline which follow a doctor giving self-publicity, although this is always a serious problem, but I was concerned about giving hope to many addicts and then not being in a position to meet that hope.

In addition to the necessity for clear scientific validation, and not just anecdotal evidence, I was increasingly convinced that it would not be enough to find a cure for the detoxification of addictions; the condition was so complex, so rooted in the family and society, that the problem of successful rehabilitation would have to be faced and overcome. The 19-nation Council of Europe Report on the prevalence of addictions had recently been published, and they had concluded 'in all countries there has been an upsurge in the number of drug dependents which has now attained the dimensions of an epidemic', and went on to state:

> It is important to have in mind that this subject includes not only psychological and medical but also social, educational, cultural and political aspects. The increase in the dimensions of the problem can be looked upon as a symptom that there is something very wrong with society.
> The problem is a problem neither of youth nor one of drugs, but a problem of a whole society and an entire lifestyle shared by young and old alike.

So, the cure of addiction involved a revolution in society, according to one of its own reputable bodies. Nineteen nations of Europe were admitting that their societies were 'sick', with 'something very wrong', and that there was a need for change in 'an entire lifestyle of a whole society'. That was revolution, and George's eyes lit up at the thought of the challenge. This is where he had come in, all those years ago. He thought that he had lost the way with the collapse of his satellite vision. Now, here we had been handed by God the possibility of changing the world in a better way than any satellite or communications system.

If I could detoxify any addict within ten days or so, then we would require a totally new psychotherapy—a spiritually based psychotherapy—to replace the failed psychotherapies of Jung and Freud and the Behaviorists. All it needed was brains and courage—and God had given us both. We also needed money, of course, but that was God's problem.

George's task now—when he wasn't shopping and cooking, etc.—was to investigate the weaknesses of the existing psychotherapies, and then to create a whole new structured treatment system based on Judaic-Christian values. My task would be to scientifically validate the detoxification process beyond all argument. If that could be accomplished to the satisfaction of all those nations with an 'epidemic' of drugs caused by 'sick societies' on their hands, then my NeuroElectric Therapy (NET) could be followed up by George's spiritual psychotherapy. Once more God had brought together our respective vocations in a unique and memorable way.

Two events helped them forward. Norman Stone, our film producer friend, was asked by the BBC in 1975 to do a film about my work, and I said if the British Medical Association approved I would be happy to cooperate, for I knew that Norman would treat the subject responsibly. He found an addict with a ten-year heroin and methadone addiction who had not been to me for treatment and knew nothing of NeuroElectric Therapy, and the television team filmed him under treatment every day. My agreement was that if the treatment failed under such close observation then I would have the failure analysed. In the event, despite the patient being under the strain of constant observation by the television team, it was strikingly successful as the cameras recorded his startling recovery on the fourth day onwards. The film was entitled *Off the Hook*, and was shown in the autumn of 1975.

The second event took place also in the latter part of 1975, and it was to shake the scientific world and provide a formidable basis for my own treatment process.

- 7 -
The Word Spreads—Treating Famous Rock Stars

*I*n September, 1975, in my old university of Aberdeen in Scotland, two scientists, Dr Hans Kosterlitz and his assistant, Dr John Hughes, announced a breakthrough which had a dramatic impact on the world-wide scientific community. Dr Kosterlitz, my former tutor in biochemistry, and Dr Hughes demonstrated the body's natural opiate substance which attached to receptor sites on brain cells to be 'enkephalin' (meaning 'inside the brain').

I had been aware from the beginning of my interest in electrical stimulation that it was not just the current directly applied to the nerve pathways which was effecting the curative process of NET. The first clue for me had been the ten-minute delay in response to the application of the treatment. From this and other observations I had become convinced that some form of chemical was being produced or released by the electrical stimulation. In my discussions with colleagues I usually referred to this as 'Chemical X'.

A few years earlier two American researchers had created a great deal of interest by demonstrating the presence of opiate receptors in the mid-brain. This indicated, in turn, the possibility of the body having a natural substance of its own which would attach to those receptors. It was this substance that Kosterlitz and Hughes had now discovered, and the treatment of addiction would be radically changed for ever because of it.

I went to Aberdeen to visit Dr Kosterlitz, to discuss his

and my own researches, and the possibility that there was a direct connection between electrical stimulation and enkephalin as the mysterious chemical I was encountering. I understood that enkephalin was to pain and emotion what adrenaline was to fight and flight, and this would explain the responses I was having. When the body was faced with some circumstance of psychological or spiritual stress, or physiological injury, it called on its enkephalin-producing mechanism to help counter the stress or injury, as it did when it required adrenaline.

Dr Kosterlitz said that although he did not know of any direct connection between electrical stimulation and the production of enkephalin, he suggested a few researchers who were working in the fields of electrical stimulation, analgesia and the opioids whose findings indicated the possibility of some association.

I returned to London more excited than ever with my research. It was a whole new world we were entering, and we had been given a crude map and a compass to discover its—literally!—mind-boggling treasures. From the point where information entered the mind by means of electrical impulses, to the deepest areas of the mind now being found to be affected in some way by electrical stimuli, a new world of health experience was being opened up. Millions in bondage to ignorance as well as chemicals could be set free. One well-known American scientist, Dr Derek Stubbs, declared:

'The language of the brain is frequency. Some of the implications of this statement are beginning to be understood. Some observations we do not yet understand. When we learn to speak the frequency language of the brain, we may begin to learn what it is saying.'

It seemed to me, therefore, that it was reasonable to assume the frequencies of my NeuroElectric Therapy (NET) were stimulating the body's own enkephalin-producing cells as only one among a wider group of natural body substances still to be discovered. Enkephalin was a narcotic, or pain-killing, substance; but there would be similar substances for alcohol, tranquillisers, stimulants like cocaine, and so on, with appropriate receptors on cell membranes responsive to respective frequencies.

What could now be postulated was that when a synthetic chemical—such as alcohol, or opium, or cocaine, or nicotine—was introduced into the body for reasons of stress or other causes, the body picked up the message by means of its own detection and data transmission system, and reduced its own natural production of the substance accordingly. This reduction, in turn, produced a drug hunger requiring another intake of the synthetic substance, and so on in an ever-increasing cycle of addiction. As the intake of the chemical increased so did the measure of the consequent drug hunger—and the more severe became the subsequent withdrawal symptoms.

What I reckoned my NET was doing was stimulating the endorphinergic neurones to produce the endorphins (meaning 'endogenous morphine') or enkephalins—and the other substances, respectively—thereby reducing the drug hunger, diminishing the withdrawal symptoms, and enabling the body to function normally once again.

I now had the strong scientific basis on which to build the NET treatment process, not only for addictions but also for other hitherto intractable conditions which were neurotransmitter-related and which could be affected by electrical stimulation—such as the paralysis diseases. But that would come later; for the present I would concentrate on the collection of the necessary data derived from clinical trials which would finally establish the treatment beyond doubt.

It was essential, therefore, for us to set up our own clinic where these studies could take place under skilled supervision of trained staff. When we had set up our charity, FREE!, we had this in mind, but in making tentative enquiries about what was involved in establishing a clinic we had been informed that what we wanted to do was not permitted under the aegis of FREE! As a fund-raising organisation governed by charity regulations in Britain, FREE! was not allowed to run medical clinics. To do this would mean setting up a separate, non-profit, organisation, with appropriate articles of association, to allow us to function as we planned. It would also take another thousand pounds in lawyers' fees.

We had exhausted the money donated by Dick and Pamela Knight, and the money from the music industry had gone into the progressive development of my NET stimulators. I had been reluctant to take patients because the time spent treating them meant that I could not pursue my research. I not only had to visit libraries and hold discussions in Britain, but search for material and visit places conducting bio-electrical investigations in Europe. Russia and the Eastern European countries had been concentrating on exploring electrical stimulation potentials since the 1930s, and they provided me with invaluable materials. Every item of new information had to be incorporated into my own NET stimulator, and constantly refined, and only then applied to the patients to evaluate their responses.

This left George to do the fund-raising—as well as the housekeeping! He wrote hundreds of letters, and arranged hundreds of meetings, in order to raise the money to keep me going. But it was heart-breaking work, because of the lack of enthusiasm for contributing to anything to do with addictions. The government departments continued to be useless, not only showing no interest in my work but also showing little or no interest in the problem of drug addiction. The only time they acted was when there was a death of a member of a prominent family, or a series of articles in the media, and there would be a flurry of cosmetic activities which quickly died away.

The irony was that other governments were showing a keen interest in my work, even sending doctors and patients to me for advice and treatment. The Iranian embassy would have provided me with a steady number of patients because of the enormity of the drug problem in Iran. I had successfully treated a member of the royal family, and this generated tremendous interest in my work. I had patients and visits from South America, Scandinavia, Hong Kong, Thailand, Australia, all anxious to introduce my treatment into their countries.

I even had a Muslim-Marxist revolutionary from Lebanon who was referred to me after I had successfully treated the son of one of the Middle East's wealthiest oil magnates. After the son was cured he told his friend, the Lebanese revolutionary, and he travelled to London for treatment. Both Lebanese had girlfriends studying at the Sorbonne University in Paris, and the two girls had been adamant that they would not get married until both their fiancés had come off drugs. The detoxification of the second Lebanese was not difficult, but like his friend and so many drug addicts he had relationship problems with his father. In our discussions with him we pointed out that the cause of his addiction was the hatred he had for his father, and the consequences of this attitude; and that the only cure for hatred was forgiveness. On one occasion his fiancée was present and she said, 'That is true. I told you, you have always found it easier to hate than to love.'

It was in these discussions that George was in his element. His knowledge of politics, and religions, and his wide experience of human nature, meant that he could meet their arguments and evasions. He was different from any psychiatrist they had ever met. When I was asked to treat the son and heir of a well-known aristocratic family who had been on so many drugs he was considered mentally damaged—he was in a mental institution when his father came to plead with me to treat him—he responded to the treatment within a few weeks, and the father was so impressed with George's hard-hitting condemnation of his relationship with his son that he invited him down to his country seat for the weekend for further intimate discussions.

I also had one of London's leading drug dealers come to me for treatment. He had been so impressed by the cure of one of his 'clients' that he got one of my patients to 'borrow' one of my machines. Then he made an appointment to see me and asked for treatment, saying that he wanted to get away from the drug scene and start a new life. I told him that I was too busy, and anyway I had no spare machines at that time. He opened a plastic bag he was carrying, took out one of my machines, and showed me his day's 'take' from drug-dealing—£25,000 in cash! He was such a charming and shameless rogue that I agreed to treat him, and after he was treated he went abroad and returned to a different career.

At the same time, as emergencies, I was treating prostitutes, criminals, runaways and other social outcasts referred to me by despairing families or caring voluntary agencies.

Over the years it had been our custom to hold Bible studies in our home for friends and neighbours, and we did the same in London. The format varied according to the individuals who came, and in London these included Brian and Betty Mawhinney, Brian and Rachel Griffiths, Os and Jenny Guinness, Nigel and Gilly Goodwin, Jim Punton and others. The studies were kept relevant by relating them to the different circumstances being experienced by the variety of professions represented by the participants.

Before the studies, we always shared a meal together, and at one of them somebody—in response to some radical proposal by George—asked Sean, our second son, 'Are you going to be a revolutionary like your father?' Sean replied sardonically, 'He hasn't left us anything to rebel against.'

But he and Lorne must have learned something about rebellion. Their school, in teaching civics, held a mock Parliament in which selected students stood for election, conducted campaigns and sought votes for their respective parties. Lorne was a Maoist-Marxist, and Sean an anarchist. Sean won—and cheerfully dissolved the whole election process!

On another occasion George and I were called to the school by the Principal to discuss Myrrh's distressing propensity for lying. It appeared that she had given colourful accounts of places she had been, and events in which she had participated, that had exceeded permitted youthful exaggerations. What had precipitated matters requiring our interview was that Myrrh had said that she could not join a school outing requiring some payment, by claiming that her parents could not afford it; while at the same time saying that our family was going on holiday to a villa in Tunisia with a private swimming pool!

We explained to the disconcerted but fascinated Principal that all Myrrh had been saying was true, we had lived that kind of life, that I was treating famous rock stars, that on other occasions we had no money—and that the wealthy family of a grateful patient had provided us with a holiday in their luxury villa in Tunisia.

But I was not yet ready to launch the treatment nationally. The theory would stand up to expert scrutiny now, but my stimulator was complex and difficult to use without adequate knowledge of all the factors involved. We needed a clinic where I would have fully trained staff to demonstrate, as a model of what could be done to solve the drug problem world-wide.

Early in 1977 Norman Stone, our film producer friend, proposed doing a follow-up film to *Off the Hook* for the BBC. Two years had passed since the first film had been made, and it was thought that another filmed account should be done to show what had happened to the addict portrayed in *Off the Hook*, and what was happening to the NET treatment.

I was happy to agree, if for no other reason than that I knew the addict concerned had recovered and was holding a steady job. The first film had been a 'diary' format of a daily record of events, and Norman wanted to change this in the second film.

The former addict was understandably reluctant to

appear in the second film, for he had made many new friends who did not know of his past, and he was building a thriving small business which might be adversely affected. But he also wanted to repay some of the help given to him in whatever way would help us and the treatment, so he agreed to co-operate.

While the film was being made I received an urgent telephone call from Canada: would I treat urgently and secretly Keith Richards of the Rolling Stones rock music group? (I use his name because, like Eric Clapton, he has spoken publicly about his treatment.)

I was not too surprised by the call, for I had already been approached on a few occasions by the Rolling Stones organisation about possible treatment for Keith, after I had treated Eric, but they had never followed through on the initial calls. This time the situation was drastically different.

Keith had been arrested in Canada, during a tour there, with a large amount of heroin in his room; consequently, instead of just being charged with possession, he was being held on the much more serious crime of drug trafficking, which could draw a sentence of twenty years' imprisonment or more. To make matters worse, the Rolling Stones on this same tour had been involved in a widely publicised, politically sensitive scandal, when the wife of the Canadian Prime Minister, Margaret Trudeau, was alleged to have spent several hours with members of the Rolling Stones in their hotel rooms. It precipitated a crisis in the relationship between the Prime Minister and his wife, and was an explosive issue between the political parties in government. To add to the seriousness of it all, the drug problem was also a major political as well as social issue at the time, and heavier penalties were being demanded for arrested drug abusers and traffickers. It was thought that public sentiment would demand that the notorious international 'bad boy' Keith Richards be given the harshest possible sentence as a deterrent to others.

Further, while this would be a personal tragedy for

Keith, it would also mean professional and financial disaster for the Rolling Stones group and organisation. For it was widely recognised in the rock music world that the key musician of the Rolling Stones was not their jet-setting singer, Mick Jagger, but the composer-guitarist Keith Richards. With Keith in prison the break-up of the long-lasting Rolling Stones was inevitable. This might not mean much to those who did not like the Rolling Stones anyway, either for their type of music or their public anti-social posturing; but, to the Stones organisation, and its associated record companies, it meant at that time a possible loss in the region of twenty million dollars.

That was what had made the call to me urgent and important. But there were also other critical problems linked with the treatment of Keith from my point of view. Keith was out on bail, and the terms of the bail restricted him to the continent of North America. Even if that could be waived by a clever lawyer (and that was unlikely, for Keith had a record of jumping bail for similar offences in other countries), he could not be treated in England (partly for tax reasons—as a tax exile he was allowed only a limited time in the UK—and partly because I had nowhere to treat him). I was not prepared to take on the treatment of such a reputedly difficult drug addict in one of his own places where he could effectively control the situation. The most difficult problem of all, of course, was that if—as I suspected—the treatment of his addiction would be used as part of a defence lawyer's plea for leniency for Keith, then I would have to be prepared to go into the witness-box and, under cross-examination by sceptical interrogators, declare my personal belief that my treatment had cured Keith's notorious drug addiction. I was happy to be judged by my peers; but being judged by prejudiced lawyers and politicians and journalists seeking to further their careers over the body of Keith and my reputation was another matter altogether.

Needless to say, the last problem bothered me the least.

As a doctor, the patient was my primary responsibility; and the issue was whether, despite the overwhelming problems, I could cure him. I had already appeared in several court cases in England on behalf of drug addicts, and I had satisfied sceptical magistrates.

It was the 'control' aspect which bothered me most. How was I to treat a temperamental, notoriously 'wild' and glamorised rock star over a period of six weeks without anyone knowing about it, without his walking out in a blaze of world publicity in a fit of pique because of what George and I would be saying to him, and without my treatment and reputation being damaged as a consequence?   I talked it over with George and we arrived at a possible solution.

We had a very good doctor friend, Dr Joe Winston, whom we had known in Hong Kong, who was now living near Philadelphia in the United States. I had communicated with Joe about my work over the years so he was well-informed about it. I could not practise in the United States, but if he would act as consultant, and find a suitable location for treatment, then that would solve one problem. We had another friend, Shorty Yeaworth, who lived about an hour's journey away from Joe in a large and isolated farmhouse, who might be willing to have Keith to stay in his home for the treatment period. Shorty and his wife, Jean, were film producers and musicians, and they had worked with drug addicts in the past.

Joe telephoned back to say that a colleague, Dr Dick Corbett, who was in charge of a leading government drug treatment unit in New Jersey, had agreed to cooperate in the treatment of Keith, but that he was sceptical about my treatment because he had been treating drug addicts for many years and could not accept that NET was so effective. Dick and Joe would draw up the necessary protocol for treatment by them which the US Government required, and which could be submitted to the Canadian authorities at a later date. Any violation of the protocol would mean the termination of the agreement, and the Rolling Stones people would have to be aware of the seriousness of this commitment.

All we had to do now was slip away from England for six weeks without raising any suspicions or awkward questions! It was not too difficult with family and friends, and with professional colleagues, who knew we had to keep the identities of our patients secret, but we had a real problem with the BBC film team. Not only had they a tight schedule to keep, but also Norman was a close friend. We decided, finally, to tell Norman that we had been called away to treat a patient for six weeks whose name must be kept secret. Norman appreciated the need for secrecy, so he arranged to postpone the film and carry on with the shooting of another film he had planned.

We arranged for a family friend to live in the flat with Sean and Myrrh (Lorne was about to start his studies as a psychiatric nurse, and as he already knew quite a bit about NET he was coming with us to help with the treatment of Keith), and we were met at the Philadelphia airport by Joe and his wife, Arlita. Keith and his common-law wife, Anita (whom I had insisted either had to come off drugs at the same time, or to stay away while he was having treatment), arrived shortly afterwards at the same airport in their private jet, accompanied by the Rolling Stones lawyer, Bill Carter.

When they appeared in the airport reception area they were accompanied by their seven-year-old son, Marlon, who was almost as notorious as Keith for his behaviour— including taking drugs and alcohol in public. Keith and Anita were floating somewhere on Cloud Nine with drugs, and Marlon was shouting and beating on them for attention. Keith, pale and haggard as always, was dressed in a white suit and purple shirt, and he stood unsmiling beside an equally sullen Anita while Bill Carter, embarrassingly, said that Keith had told him to send me and the doctors off, cancel the arrangements, and to prepare to leave for New York right away.

I took a deep breath, then slowly and clearly spelled it

out to the red-faced lawyer: either they get into the car right away, and get on with the treatment as agreed, or we would immediately inform the authorities—and Keith and Anita would never see New York, as they would be on the plane back to Canada and prison. They might as well learn right now that I was in charge, and that they would have to do exactly as I said. I was here to cure their addictions, not to play silly games at the drug-induced whim of arrogant and temperamental celebrities.

The matter was settled when it was discovered that their son had already left the airport with Arlita and her son, Sam, in the Winston car.

When we got to Shorty and Jean Yeaworth's home Keith and Anita were still so high on drugs they did not want to eat. I attached the machines to them, with the usual instructions, then we all left them. When Joe and Dick arrived the next day they were still sleeping. Anita was restless, but more because of a huge thigh abscess—from her drug injections—than anything else.

Keith slept for forty-three hours, and, when he finally awoke, clear-eyed and refreshed, Dick Corbett the sceptic had become an amazed convert. He had never seen anything like it. He had seen Keith arrive under the influence of drugs beyond anything in his experience; he had confirmed this with urine tests he had done, he had taken Keith's case-history himself as chief-of-protocol for the US authorities, and from his experience he was aware of what Keith should have been like without the NET treatment. Later Keith himself was to say in an interview:

'It's so simple it's not true. It's a little metal box with leads that clip on to your ears, and in two or three days— which is the worst period for kicking junk—it leaves your system.'

It took more than that, of course. Over the next three weeks there were times when things got very rough indeed, especially when George was having to deal with the underlying causes of addiction as they applied to Keith and the lifestyle of the Rolling Stones. At one point, Keith threw his radio across the garden in fury when George ordered him to turn off the blaring rock music while they were having a discussion. But he certainly quickly lost the awful haggard look and even started to look tanned and healthy from sitting in the lovely gardens.

When Mick Jagger came to visit him he said unbelievingly that he hadn't seen Keith look so well for ten years. Ahmed Ertegun, the head of Atlantic Records—who had provided me with research funds in the past—also visited Keith and was so impressed he offered to raise funds for the treatment to be introduced into the United States. But Keith's increasing restlessness was a problem, and even in our isolated farmhouse there were dealers seeking to provide him with drugs—at extortionate rates, of course.

Apart from the drug dealers we were confident that the media and others knew nothing of our whereabouts, until one day Shorty, after answering the telephone, said that Norman Stone and Steve Turner were in Washington to make a film and were on their way to see him in a couple of hours. Shorty knew them, and had been unable to think up a good reason to discourage their visit. We accepted the fact that they had known about Eric Clapton, and had kept it confidential, and would no doubt be prepared to do the same with Keith.

Their faces were a study when they arrived and saw us, and Keith, sitting there. Their film assignment was about black gospel music, and they had been visiting Nashville among other places, interviewing people known to Keith, so they were able to talk music gossip with him. It was not possible to film Keith himself, but Norman arranged a filmed interview with Dick Corbett at his drug clinic to discuss his views about NET and the treatment of his present unidentified patients. Dick confirmed that he was in touch with the government regarding the treatment process, and that he was recommending that NET be introduced into the United States.

After three weeks at Shorty and Jean's for the detox programme we decided that Keith could leave and have the remaining three weeks in his own rented home, with anonymous access to a local Philadelphia studio where he could work with Mick Jagger on some recording ideas. On the day he left there was a convoy of limousines to take Keith, Marlon their son, and some of the Atlantic Records personnel to their home. I found it very moving, after all the struggles of the past three weeks, to see the tough, saturnine Keith give Jean Yeaworth a warm hug with his 'thank you' for their hospitality—and then turn to George, give him a hug, and say smilingly, 'Take care, you b°°°°°.'

When the black stretch limousine pulled away, on the window-ledge at the rear there was conspicuously displayed the supposedly uncontrollable Marlon's personal Sunday school presentation copy of the Bible—which he had been given while attending with the Winstons' son. He had refused to allow it to be packed because he wanted to be certain that it went with him!

When Keith's treatment was successfully completed, and the medical report submitted to the US authorities by Dick and Joe, I went to Washington for a meeting with Dr Peter Bourne, one of President Jimmy Carter's top three White House advisers. I had met him in the past at some international conferences on addiction, but he was now in a position to use considerably more influence. When we met him only a few doors away from the President's Oval Office he showed us around while we talked. He said that I would have to go through the usual procedures for official approval in the United States, such as submitting detailed studies of my research to the Food and Drug Administration, but that he would give me introductions to key people.

It now looked as if there was a greater possibility of my work being recognised in the United States than in Britain, and George and I discussed the implications of moving there. Neither of us were particularly happy at the prospect, for although we had many good friends and enjoyed being there for short periods, the thought of living there for several years did not attract us at all. Also, I was reluctant to break completely with Britain because of the work I had so painstakingly done there over the past few years, and the interest and respect of some of my professional peers. However, I realised that if there was no funding forthcoming in Britain then my work could well disappear, and in the light of that possibility it was better that I look to the United States.

With the return of a cured and visibly healthy Keith Richards to Canada to face his trial, secrecy was no longer necessary and it was in the Rolling Stones' interest to give his successful cure as much publicity as possible. In the full glare of the media our six-week treatment protocol agreed with the US authorities was produced as evidence of the *bona fides* of the professional medical personnel concerned, and Keith was cleared of all charges. This produced a series of articles—usually misleading, as NET was mistakenly described either as 'electroacupuncture' or 'electric shock therapy'—across the world about 'Doctor Meg's' successful treatment of famous drug-addicted rock stars. I was not happy with this publicity as I was still not ready to release the NET treatment on a national or international level.

Despite this media interest, when we returned to London we found nothing there to encourage our remaining in Britain—if anything, such popular publicity simply stiffened the resistance of the establishment psychiatrists and government officials against me, so we gave notice to our landlord that we were terminating our lease of the Harley Street flat at the end of July, 1977. This would cut our links with Britain for some time. Ironically, the 26th of that same month was scheduled for the showing of Norman's second BBC filmed investigation of my work, entitled *Still Off the Hook*, right after the main nine o'clock news. The final scene showed us packing up our belongings into two lots—one for the United States, and one to be stored until we returned to Britain—and the door closing.

The film was shown on a Sunday night, and after a celebratory party we left the following morning for Scotland, where we had arranged to live with George's sister, Margaret, until we had definite word from the United States.

We stopped at several places en route, some for the children's interest and some professional meetings for me. When we finally arrived at Lenzie, outside Glasgow, where George's sister lived, there were several urgent messages waiting for us. The most urgent was from Norman, who wanted us to know that, following the showing of the film, there had been many enquiries, but three were of particular importance: one from the Rank Foundation, one from the director of the Rowntree Trust, and one from the Sir Halley Stewart Medical Trust. All were interested in helping me in some way. Could I telephone them immediately?

When I did I found that each of them wanted to know what they could do to keep my treatment in the country. The chairman of the Rank Foundation—Major Robin Cowen, son-in-law of the founder, Lord Rank—was especially concerned, and said that he would be willing to come up to Scotland immediately to discuss with me what the Rank Foundation could do to help. Richard Rowntree of the Rowntree Trust was also concerned to do something, although his was a social and not a medical Trust. The Sir Halley Stewart Medical Trust was founded to help with pioneering forms of medicine, and the secretary was anxious to know if they could do anything to help. It was almost an embarrassment of riches after the poverty of possibilities of the past few years.

They were all true to their promises. Major Cowen came to Lenzie and spent several hours discussing what would be required to keep me and the treatment in England at this stage. I told him that we would need a clinic for the necessary clinical trials to establish the new form of treatment, and probably about £100,000 for the first year of operation. He said that he would have to consult his fellow trustees, but he thought it possible they would approve. However, something on this scale would take several months to discuss and decide, and what would we do in the meantime?

The problem solved itself. Dick Corbett telephoned to say that there was an unexpected delay because the new Carter administration had recently introduced legislation limiting the employment of foreign doctors, and their proposed three-year invitation to me would require a special Congressional amendment to that legislation, which would take time. Then, Richard Rowntree also came to Lenzie with a colleague and offered to provide me with sufficient interim support until the Rank Foundation decided what they could do. The Sir Halley Stewart Medical Trust offered to provide funding for a laboratory research study.

So, once again we were on the move, looking for yet another temporary home somewhere in the south of England; or, at least, somewhere near London. I had decided that what we required for our new type of detoxification and rehabilitation clinic was a large, but not too large, residential building, *not* institutional, which would take about twenty patients. It would have to be near London so that I could keep in touch with my research and other responsibilities; but far enough away from London so that addicts would be discouraged from attempting a run to the city to seek drugs. I had a vague mental image of the sort of place I wanted so that I would know it if I saw it, but it would mean travelling around the countryside looking at possibilities.

This would be the first fully integrated addiction treatment unit. There were individual treatment centres, rehabilitation centres, information centres, therapeutic centres, detoxification centres, but there was no single unit incorporating all aspects.

We found a temporary cottage in which to live for the present outside the village of Cowden, in Kent. Once again we hired a removal van and filled it with our tea-boxes of books and research notes, which was all we possessed. It was November, 1977—five years almost to the day since I had first started investigating NeuroElectric Therapy in Hong Kong. George had said it would take me at least five years, and it looked as if there were still a number of years ahead.

I concentrated on developing a new, up-to-date fourth model of NET stimulator which would be the definitive model for the clinical trials. There were several major technical difficulties in my specific bio-electrical formulae, which were becoming more complex as I unravelled the secrets of the body's own electro-magnetic information data transmission system. But eventually a mutual friend introduced me to Peter Loose, who had a small company, European Electronic Systems, who said he could meet my necessary demands. His company had no knowledge of medical devices, being an audio-visual facility, but he was prepared to help me as a fellow Christian. He and I together visited Dr John Bates of the National Hospital for Nervous Diseases in Queen's Square, London, and received much sound advice for the model from him.

George had to produce a series of lectures for the nurses and counsellors we would be using at the clinic, based on his former experiences with addicts of all kinds in different countries and cultures. His intimate journalistic knowledge of various forms of treatment facilities in Hong Kong and the United States, with their known weaknesses, was now invaluable as we constructed a format of our own. I had to draft a variety of papers—medical questionnaires, case-history forms, treatment sheets, licence requests, technical data reports—for the new project, as this was a totally new enterprise.

- 8 -

Getting Involved in International Politics

Is that what you're looking for?' said George, passing over the newspaper. He indicated an advertisement halfway down the page.

I looked at the picture of an Elizabethan Tudor house set in a sweep of lawns, and went on to read the details. It was the kind of place we had been searching for all year, and I looked up to see George smiling knowingly.

'Two hundred thousand pounds,' I said noncommittally.

'A mere bagatelle,' George waved it away. ' "The cattle on a thousand hills are God's." The question is: do you like it well enough to take the next step to having a look at it?'

'I seem to remember playing this scene before,' I replied drily.

An hour later we were driving through the glorious Sussex countryside looking for Broadhurst Manor. We almost missed it, had almost given up the hunt in a network of country lanes, when we found the turn-off leading to the driveway, and it was there in front of us.

We stopped the car at the end of the drive and, speechless, gazed through the windscreen at the weather-beaten, E-shaped, Elizabethan manor house, framed between the tall, Italian wrought-iron gates at the end of a long avenue of lime trees, its soaring lines softened by climbing green and bronze ivy and pale mauve wisteria.

'This is it,' I breathed, entranced.

Beside me, George took a long breath. 'This we must

have,' he said. 'The place, the setting, the atmosphere, is just right.'

The 300-year-old Tudor manor was located in a dip in the rolling Sussex Downs, with a dark wood behind a chain of four small lakes running through the tree-studded gardens. The leaded, mullioned windows on all sides, glinting in the morning sun, looked out on different scenes of breath-taking loveliness. Far off, sheep bleated plaintively, orchestrating with the musical birdsong.

'Two hundred thousand pounds,' I repeated pensively, 'How are we going to find that kind of money?' For although the Rank Foundation had decided they would help us fund a place for a clinic, they had not mentioned the price they were prepared to pay; but it seemed reasonable to suppose they were thinking in the region of a hundred thousand pounds at the most.

'For a desirable residence,' George said dreamily, 'with a former Prime Minister of Britain as a next-door neighbour.'

'Who?' I asked sceptically, thinking he was joking.

'Harold Macmillan,' George replied. 'We passed his place at the end of the road as we drove in. We will just have to take this a step at a time,' he continued thoughtfully, 'and the next step is to ask George Fox, the Rank representative, to come down for a visit and see what he thinks of the place—without, of course, mentioning the price to him until afterwards.'

We went to the estate agents and got the sale brochures giving more details. The photographs of the interior of the manor showed rooms and vistas of a size and quality which confirmed us in our determination to have the house if at all possible. The present owners of the property had only lived in the manor since the beginning of the century, but there had been a house on the spot since Roman times: the first Broadhurst Manor was mentioned in the Domesday Book in 1086. I telephoned George Fox, the surveyor and adviser to the Rank Foundation, and arranged for him to see the brochures. When he agreed to visit the house I breathed a sigh of relief; at least we had passed the first obstacle.

The inside of the manor, when we visited, was warm, with polished oak panelling and great open inglenook fireplaces in which logs burned fragrantly. Oak staircases and narrow well-lit corridors linked the roomy but not too large bedrooms into an attractive and manageable single unit so that it had the right residential, and not institutional, feel about it that I wanted. However, the reception rooms were large, and this was excellent for the purposes which I had in mind.

I watched George Fox furtively as he went round inspecting the things surveyors do, and when we got outside I asked him anxiously what he thought.

He nodded appreciatively. 'Very, very nice,' he said. 'And in first-class condition, too. Have you any idea what the asking price is?'

It was the question I dreaded. 'Two hundred thousand pounds,' I said hesitantly.

'Are you sure?' he asked, surprised. 'I would have thought it was more than that. It is a very reasonable price for what we have here. I just sold a smaller and less attractive place for a much higher price last week.'

'But will Rank consider buying it for us at that price?' I asked doubtfully.

'Well, we won't know that until we ask, will we?' George Fox replied laughingly. 'I'll give Robin Cowen a ring tonight and find out if they want me to do any more about it. It will have to go before the Trustees, of course, but he will give me some indication on the phone.'

The word from Major Cowen was to go ahead with negotiations, and we began excitedly the many preparations for setting up the new clinic. Everything from shopping to schools for the children, from furniture auctions to transport, from availability of staff to organising appropriate supervisory committees, from ordering printed letterheads to completing training manuals, had to be done by ourselves.

Some of it we had started, but most of it could not be pushed forward until we knew the size and whereabouts of the clinic, and its potential. I estimated that Broadhurst Manor would provide twenty beds for patients, in addition to basic staff, and that because of the specialised nature of the detoxification and rehabilitation in treating addictions we would need about twenty nursing and administrative personnel to run the clinic.

There were also other unknown factors to be taken into consideration, such as local prejudice against treating addictions in a prestigious area. From the staffing point of view, the village, Horsted Keynes, was about two miles away with the nearest public transport; Haywards Heath, the nearest town, was six miles to the south; London was forty-five miles away by road, and about an hour by train. Finally, there were the known difficulties of obtaining official permits to transform a listed historical building such as Broadhurst Manor into a medical clinic for an unrecognised treatment process such as NET. And all of this had to be successfully completed before the clincal trials were even begun.

By the time the negotiations were completed it was late August, 1978, and the temporary lease of our cottage in Cowden was due to expire at the end of the month. There seemed to be no problem, however, for we were scheduled to take possession of Broadhurst Manor at the end of August. But the owner's aged mother, who had not wanted her son to sell the manor, proved obstreperous, and she began a campaign of delays. Under the existing law she had only to stay on in the house indefinitely after the other members of the family left, and there was nothing we could do about it.

When we vacated the cottage in Cowden at the end of August we had no place to live, and we hurriedly arranged for the children to stay with friends in London while we found a small, short-term rental in Haywards Heath. Lorne was living in the nurses' quarters at the hospital where he was training as a psychiatric nurse. We waited impatiently through September, working as best as we could out of suitcases, for we had had to put our tea-chests of research books and notes into storage until we could legally enter the manor. What made it even worse was that we had naturally arranged for all mail to be sent to us at the manor after August, and we had no access to that mail now—some of it important and urgent—because the old lady refused to talk to her own family, and denied that any mail was arriving.

The winter approached and what warm clothing we had was in storage. Our short-term rental ended and we had to find other living quarters. In desperation George answered a local advertisement in a Christian journal offering accommodation for 'elderly retired couple'. It was in a large roomy house in the country about ten miles south of Haywards Heath, with its surrounding fields rented to a thoroughbred horse-breeder. Its owners were a pleasant Christian couple, with a teenage family, who had thought the rooms could be rented to an elderly retired couple now that their children were away at boarding schools. After the initial surprise at our particular request they agreed to rent to us until we got into Broadhurst Manor.

Meanwhile, we had another major problem on our hands. The Rank purchase of the historic Broadhurst Manor as a clinic for drug and alcohol addicts had been widely reported, especially in local papers. This had created an outcry in the village parish of Horsted Keynes, and the parish council protested—rightly, in our opinion, if it were true—that the district council had not consulted with them, or informed them, about the project.

Public meetings were held in the village hall, and letters of protest were signed. The newspapers took up the issue and our names, photographs and work soon were a regular feature as the issue escalated. George was delighted, for the publicity generated pressures on everybody concerned and exposed the real problems of addiction lying at the roots of society—the family, social and political prejudices—which had to be overcome if the problem was ever to be solved.

We had done everything correctly, as required by law, but it appeared that there were local political issues and personality clashes, and we were in the centre of these clashes. Finally, George decided, in the interests of good relations, to offer to attend a public meeting in the Horsted Keynes village hall to meet with the villagers, to show the BBC films about our work, and to take questions from those concerned.

The night of the meeting the village hall was packed, with scores of people crowded around the walls and doorway and spilling into the street outside. A representative of the Rank Foundation was there—so were the Press!—and George and I were on the platform with the local council members.

The chairman of the council was courteous and firm, pointing out that we were not guilty of any misdemeanors, that we had properly observed all requirements in our presentation and negotiations, and that we had volunteered to attend the public meeting of our own free will. It was almost the only courtesy for the next two or three hours, as individuals with personal or political prejudices questioned, hectored, orated and shouted their objections to treating drug addicts and alcoholics in their neighbourhood. It was as nasty an exhibition of antisocial, let alone unchristian, conduct that it was possible to find.

In the midst of it all George stood to field questions—polite, reasonable, patient, understanding, to an astonishing degree—and only occasionally lashing out with incisive rebuke or mockery when some individual was outrageously rude or selfish or prejudiced. As the hubbub gradually subsided, he skilfully isolated the few protest leaders and moved into attack on them for their antisocial attitudes, their deplorable lack of human as well as spiritual values, their absorption with selfish and material issues, until they were silenced. Then the normal, decent, sympathetic individuals took courage and let their voices be heard. Finally, the chairman closed the meeting, and gave us a warm welcome to the village and neighbourhood. We were accepted.

But there was still no sign of goodwill or movement from the old lady at Broadhurst Manor, who continued to claim sickness and any other reason for not being able to move out, leaving us very frustrated as the weeks passed into months. We could not get to our mail, and we understood that cables had been sent regarding important matters which had not been forwarded to us.

Right in the midst of the confusion I was asked by Lord Harlech if I could possibly treat the son of an internationally known family who was a serious drug addict. The family had tried everything and everybody, they knew that I had successfully treated Lord Harlech's daughter, and they pleaded with him to use his influence with me to treat their son. They had put him into a mental institution for the time being, but this was a crisis measure and very secret. The problem was further complicated by the fact that not only was the family internationally known, but one member was running for President of his country and there were political and financial implications which the international media would love to exploit. The resentful drug addict was determined to get revenge on the family by giving the media all they wanted.

I told Lord Harlech our personal domestic situation, which was made even more complicated by the fact that, even if it were agreed by the Christian family with whom we were living temporarily to have this patient under treatment in their home, they would have to know the identity of the patient. Further, it was essential in treating all drug addicts that they should be subject to firm discipline, and this would be difficult for George and me to apply because the Christian family did not have even normal family discipline in their home—and the wife dominated the husband to an embarrassing degree. Finally, the parents were Pentecostal-type Christians, whose opinions and practices we found it difficult to tolerate in normal circumstances, and which would be positively Martian-like to the proposed patient.

However, none of these objections were a hindrance to the desperate family of the drug addict, and I finally agreed to take their son (whom I shall call John, not his real name) into the Christian home with us.

He arrived—complete with official bodyguard!—and almost immediately made it clear that he had no intention of staying, that he had only agreed to come because the alternative was a mental institution, that he had every intention of suing his family just as soon as he could get hold of a telephone to call a lawyer. He was suffering from withdrawals, he smoked one cigarette after another, he swore profanely in almost every sentence, and was unbelievably rude. He was unmanageable.

There was no way in which this could be tolerated under any circumstances, and George in his inimitable manner finally spelled it out in words and phrases that rendered John speechless. George was a disciplinarian and a journalist, and he had trawled the gutters of Asia for many years; there was nothing that an immature twenty-three-year-old junkie could do to stem him in full flow. I added my own firm orders. The turning point came when the bodyguard—who had been with the family since John was a child—really worked him over, told him it was his last chance, and that if John did not grasp it his orders were to return him to the mental institution right away.

John sullenly accepted the inevitable, and submitted himself to the treatment with the minimum possible co-operation. He refused to be normally pleasant at the dining table, boorishly smoked without asking permission (until ordered by George to do so, or get outside until he learned better manners), recklessly talked about his famous family's indiscretions before the horrified Christian hosts, and mocked their religious practices.

We had been given some money to give him for special expenses such as cigarettes, but instead of buying these for him we gave him the money. We were fairly certain that he would take off as soon as he had it, and so we were not surprised when he did not turn up at meal time.

As it happened, his mother telephoned during his absence to ask how he was getting on. When I told her that he had probably gone to the nearby seaside resort of Brighton she was furious, and demanded to know what kind of doctor I was that allowed patients to wander unattended all over the country. I said, the kind of doctor that did not put children into a mental institution simply because they were a social embarrassment. That did not stop her, and eventually George, who could see I was under pressure, signalled to me to hand him the telephone. I did.

Pacing the floor, George informed her in scathing terms that her twenty-three-year-old son was an immature and uncouth lout, who had been allowed to believe he could do anything and say anything to anybody without fear of consequences, and that he was in danger of bringing death to himself and disgrace to the family because neither his father nor his mother had bothered to take the time nor make the effort to bring him up with a proper set of values. Did she expect us to do in six weeks what they had not been able to do in twenty-three years? Or, did they only want us to keep him out of the way of the media to save their own embarrassment? And so on. Both eventually cooled down and talked amicably about the treatment.

We were asleep that night when the telephone rang. George picked up the phone. It was John. I looked at the clock; it was one-thirty in the morning.

'Hello, is that you, George?' John asked brightly.

'Yes,' George said neutrally.

'George, you're not going to believe this,' John continued.

'Try me,' George said drily.

'Well, I came down to Brighton to buy some music tapes, had a few beers and a meal, went to see a film, and what do you know, I've missed the last train.'

'I can believe that,' George said reasonably.

'Yeah, well, can you pick me up?' John asked, with assumed casualness.

'No,' said George.

'No?' John's voice rose incredulously. 'What do you mean, no?'

'I mean no, I won't pick you up,' George explained patiently.

'Then how do I get back?' John demanded.

'The same way as you got there,' George replied.

'There are no trains or buses running,' John protested.

'You should have thought about that earlier,' George said, 'before you left Haywards Heath station, or at Brighton station, in the several hours you had to make the decision. That's what sensible people do.'

'It's too late for all that °°°° now,' John shouted angrily. 'Don't °°°° me around, man.'

'Take a taxi,' George suggested equably.

Silence.

'I've no money left,' John said, less confidently.

'Then hitch-hike,' George proposed. 'It's only twenty miles.'

'It's raining,' John said surlily.

'That's England,' George said understandingly. 'It was in the weather forecast, if you had listened.'

'Come on, man,' John urged, sensing a softening. 'You can be here in thirty minutes.'

'No way,' George said firmly. 'You chose not to discuss your plans with me or Meg, so now you take responsibility for your decisions. You spent your money in the way you wanted, you spent the time in the way you wanted, which is fine by me. All normal people do that. Just take the consequences, like we all do. And while you're waiting for the hitchhike, or walking back, think over whether it was worth it. That's what all non-junkies do all the time. Here endeth the first lesson. See you sometime.'

'You–'

George hung up.

It took John nearly four hours and three hitches to get back, and we let him sleep until after midday. When he finally put in an appearance it was to announce that he was leaving right away, and to telephone his family to meet him. He was through.

'Sit down, ****head,' George said coldly. 'You're not going anywhere, or doing anything. You have no money, and we're not giving you any. When you leave here you will either be cured, or you will be on your way back to the mental institution with your bodyguard. If you choose to walk away now and take the consequences, that's fine with us. We just telephone your decision to your family. We took you in to do one thing: to cure you of your addiction. You stay on that machine until Meg declares you detoxified, and you stay close to me until I say that you are fit to live with. Your problem, like all your kind, is not drugs; it's monomania.

'You are a foul-mouthed, rude, spoiled, ill-mannered, dirty, selfish and despicable lout. Meg and I are sitting here desperately trying to find ways and means to cure millions of drug addicts who want to be given a chance of a cure, and we get stuck with a rich ****head like you. Only one thing keeps me from punching your nose, throwing you out of here, and sending you back to Mummy, and that is, for some obscure reason, God sent you here to us at this time. I don't want you here, I loathe your kind and all you represent, I find you personally offensive in every way—but I'm stuck with you as somebody God loves and wants me to love as myself. Now, Meg and I will treat you on that basis: we will treat you the same as we treat our own children whom we love, but it won't be because of your name or fame or money or influence. You are here to be cured, so—get cured, or start walking. Am I understood?'

John, white-faced, swallowed, then—surprisingly—smiled. 'Yes, SIR,' he said, only half-sarcastically. 'Has anybody ever told you you're a real ******?'

'All the time, lad,' George grinned. 'Just don't ever forget it, and we'll get along all right.'

From then on George was like a sergeant-major with him. He told him to take baths, get clean clothes, if he wanted to smoke in the house to ask the hostess's permission, to hold chairs for ladies at the table. When we took the family out for an evening John went with us, and George taught him how to choose what wines to go with what food (his own so-called wealthy and aristocratic family had never bothered, he said, and all he knew about was beer—and booze to get drunk).

Once he had got over his antisocial rebellion he was a nice person, and we really enjoyed his company. When we were out one evening I felt a lump in my throat as he fetched my coat and—obviously not quite knowing what he should do to help me, but trying to be polite—just handed it to me. After six weeks or so he was ready to go home.

We met with one of the family psychiatrists first, to discuss John's future. He was a well-known public figure, and he was one of those who had committed John to a mental institution.

'All that John needs,' George said finally, 'is a family who cares for him and his real needs, and a priest who will teach him some basic spiritual values—and kick his backside when he needs it. Someone he trusts and respects.'

'Just like that?' the psychiatrist asked sceptically. 'Do you know how much money he has access to?'

'I thought we were talking about his health, not his wealth,' George replied bluntly. 'But for what it's worth, yes, I know how much money he expects, for he has told me, and he is determined to get hold of it, and to spend it.'

'And you think that's a good idea?' the psychiatrist asked sarcastically. 'What do you think will happen if it is all just handed over to him?'

'He would go on a wild spending spree,' George answered. 'He would buy cars, drugs, drink, women—and might die in three months.'

'Yet you think it's a good idea,'—the psychiatrist made it a statement, not a question.

'Yes,' George affirmed. 'I do—and not just because you've tried everything else, legal and illegal, and have failed.'

'Why, then, and on what authority?' the psychiatrist demanded, obviously nettled.

'Luke fifteen,' said George laconically.

The psychiatrist looked at him in silence, swivelled his chair to search in the bookcase, and pulled out a book.

'You probably think I am the only psychiatrist in the city to have a Bible in his bookcase,' he observed in response to the surprised look on our faces.

'You must be the only psychiatrist in the *country* to have a Bible in his office,' George commented drily. 'Do you need any help to find it?'

The psychiatrist shook his head negatively, found the chapter in the New Testament, and read the parable of the Prodigal Son through to the end. It was the story, told by Jesus, of the father who had two sons, the younger of whom asked for his inheritance right away so that he could do what he liked with it. When he got hold of it he left home and used the money in spendthrift fashion on living the high life. When his money was all gone, and his good-time friends had also disappeared, he was reduced to eating the slops of the pigs he was attending. At this low point he thought, 'What am I doing here like this when I could be working as a servant for my father?' He started for home but before he arrived there his father, who was on the lookout for him, met him and refused to employ him as a servant, saying that as his son he would be treated as his son, and restored him to the family.

The psychiatrist closed the Bible, laid it down on the desk, and turned to us, looking thoughtful.

'That's the way that Jesus says God does it,' George said quietly, 'and it never fails. If it's good enough for God, it's good enough for us. St Augustine summed it up well, when he said, "Do as you will, and pay for it." The secret, of course, is not in just suffering the consequences of one's actions, but in the constancy of the father's forgiving love for the prodigal son. For John to be really cured, and not just detoxified, both he and his family would have to read, understand and practise Luke fifteen.'

'Otherwise . . .' prompted the psychiatrist.

'Otherwise, whatever temporary help we give, he will be back on drugs again within a few weeks or months,' I answered.

But when John got home, it seemed to us, his problems were insurmountable. He had asked us if we would go with him to meet his family, and to discuss his future. He did not trust them, and we were happy that he felt he could trust us. His family were highly publicised as a family-centred group, but all that this meant was that they were seen to socialise together. We had heard from John what was really going on between the various members of the family. A great deal of John's problem lay in his objecting to what the family required in 'conforming' for the sake of appearances.

When we met all the members of the family to discuss John we had asked that he should be present, that he should be party to any decisions that affected his own life; but when we got there we found—as he had warned us—that he had not been invited at all. They were filled with admiration for what had been done with John in only six weeks—his health, his appearance, his unexpected good manners, his new reasonableness, his desire to study and work. But they weren't prepared to trust him to keep on with this. They said he should keep off drugs (although some other members of the family were also known to be taking drugs—but were not so embarrassingly public about it as John), complete his graduation at university, marry a nice girl and not cause embarrassment to the family. That was all. It looked as if they had never read Luke fifteen.

The postscript is: the family arranged for John to go to a strict foster family ('like the Pattersons,' they said!), but never visited him. As we foretold, he went back on drugs, but I learned later from his psychotherapist (who was so impressed with John's response to NET that he wanted to

send another prominent individual for addiction treatment)
that John had no real problem with drugs afterwards.
However, whenever there was a family row over some
aspect of his conduct he would go on a spree. During one
such incident, when he had been publicly humiliated by the
family, he had inadvertently overdosed on a combination of
pills and alcohol.

- 9 -
Setting Up Britain's First Combined Detox and Rehab Clinic

*A*t Christmas we had to vacate the rooms with the Christian family and so, once again, we were homeless— 'homeless at Christmas': where had we heard that before?— as the old lady was still being obdurate about moving out. Our children were still living in suitcases and difficult circumstances in London. It was Sean's final school year, with the critical university entrance examinations to be faced in June, and he had no home, no quietness, no books, for his studies.

Then some Hong Kong friends, who had a house in North London, were able to let us have the use of it for several months, and we were together as a family again. Through some friends I met Dr Williams, the Director of the Marie Curie Cancer Research Foundation, and we discussed the possibilities of my using NET in a series of experiments to deal with stress. Stress had emerged as a significant factor in cancer conditions, and any form of treatment that could help with this was of interest to the Marie Curie Foundation. We set up a research programme at the Marie Curie Institute, only an hour's drive away from Broadhurst Manor, where one of Dr Williams' researchers, Dr Ifor Capel, would be allocated to work with me on certain aspects of amelioration of stress and detoxification from drugs by means of NET on animal models.

At last, in February 1979, the old lady moved out of the manor and we were able to complete negotiations. Heavy snow was falling, thick ice made the roads dangerous, and the plunging temperature burst the pipes in the house—but we did not care. George rented a van and, lurching and skidding all over the place on the ice-covered, snow-bound, country roads, we brought our goods out of storage and began furnishing the house. When we arrived it had been stripped of everything—no cooker, not even a light bulb had been left behind. We had thirty rooms to furnish and George had been attending auction sales all over London to find appropriate furniture for our Tudor manor at as low prices as possible.

The arrangement with the Rank Foundation was that they would provide us with the financial 'pump-priming' for the first year of the experimental clinic, and that we— particularly George, through our fund-raising charity, FREE!—would try to find other sources of funding to keep it going when the year's trial was completed. In order to keep as much of the 'pump-priming' money as possible for the treatment process, the Foundation also generously agreed to pay for the basic alterations to the manor required by the authorities to change its use to a medical clinic.

While the plans for the required alterations were being processed by the authorities with the usual infuriating bureaucratic slowness, I was invited to go to the University of Pennsylvania as a visiting scientist to deliver a series of lectures on NeuroElectric Therapy. At the same time I was asked to supervise a comparative investigation of NET and methadone withdrawal at the Lakeland Drug Abuse Clinic in New Jersey, in association with Dr Dick Corbett and his staff.

I went there in April, 1979, and discovered what I suspected: that the rapid detoxification of NET created real problems for the normal slow technique of psychotherapy used in the standard rehabilitation. All forms of psycho- therapy—whether Freudian, Jungian, or Behaviourist, or an empirical mixture—were usually practised as a support system in conjunction with a diminishing of the drug of addiction; and this could vary from three weeks to three months, or even three years at times, depending on the seriousness of the addict's condition. I took all patients off whatever drug of addiction they used as soon the NET began, and this meant that they were ready for psychotherapeutic help from about the third or fourth day of treatment—sometimes earlier. It was this rapidity of recovery which caused problems at the clinic.

I was very impressed by the existing rehabilitation programme of the Lakeland Clinic being conducted by Pete Gardini, a former addict who had been cured while in prison by means of 'Synanon' techniques, and it was a variation of those techniques which were being practised at this Drug Abuse Unit. But it was admitted by Pete and the staff that these fell far short of what was possible in effective rehabilitation to follow detoxification treatment by NET.

The 'Synanon' treatment had been begun by an ex-Alcoholics Anonymous instructor called Charles, or 'Chuck', Dederich in California in the United States. In its early days this organisation was known as 'Tender Loving Care', and the name 'Synanon' only emerged later from a word used mistakenly by a drug addict who confused 'seminar' and 'symposium'. Chuck Dederich liked the hybrid word, Synanon, and it became the official name of the rapidly growing drug treatment facility.

Chuck Dederich and his early associates of recovered alcoholics and drug addicts had no basic philosophy or psychotherapeutic theory when they began in 1958. They had learned quite a bit from Alcoholics Anonymous, but they were dissatisfied with several aspects and then set out to develop their own form of treatment. Dederich and a few of his associates were well-read people and they incorporated ideas and practices from whatever they were reading at the time—from Thomas Aquinas to Ralph Waldo Emerson. These theories and practices were thrashed out at therapy sessions, which themselves grew out of confrontational discussions, and this eventually became known as 'the Synanon Game'.

The Synanon Game was a kind of no-holds-barred encounter session, usually involving about twelve or fifteen members sitting in a circle. These were very aggressive occasions, no limit being applied on verbal violence which proceeded on the basis of 'targeting individuals'. One participant would point out the weakness or defect of another, or a mistake made in some task, and then the others would zero in on that individual in an increasingly denunciatory attack. Unless a person could talk their way out of the mounting accusations by means of quick wit or verbal facility, a tidal wave of pseudo-anger would engulf him or her. When the individual could no longer withstand that emotionally draining barrage he or she would 'confess' the weaknesses, defects or mistakes, 'repent' by promising to mend their ways, and be 'forgiven' by a now warm and welcoming group. The 'target' would then shift to another individual in the group 'Game'.

This was a powerful device to help addicts break out of their self-centred, exploiting practices, by exposing the deeply entrenched lies, hypocrisies and deceits they had become accustomed to use to feed their indulgences—and which were only too well understood by the ex-alcoholic and ex-addict leaders of Synanon. The 'Game' therapy sessions became famous in the 1960s, even outside the realm of drug and alcohol treatment units, and were soon the basis of reputable rehabilitation practices not only in the United States but also in several countries across the world.

However, as the Synanon organisation became popular it became rich and powerful, and in the late 1970s rumours began to circulate of disturbing claims to being a 'new religion', of using armed security guards, of mass vasectomies, of mass mate-swapping, and other bizarre practices. When the news media reported some of these happenings, Synanon launched massive multimillion-dollar litigation suits against them, and the Synanon armed security squads became 'goon squads' beating up reporters.

Finally, in 1978, the media in the United States erupted with a report that two Synanon members had been arrested for putting a live rattlesnake into the mail-box of a lawyer who had been investigating some of Synanon's activities on behalf of a client. The two members, together with Chuck Dederich, were charged with complicity to murder the lawyer.

All of this was very interesting from a professional point of view—how could something which began by being so good and useful in drug treatment become so bad?—but it became personal to me and George through an unusual combination of circumstances.

George had a financier friend in California, Herman Kingsley, with whom he had worked while on the satellite communications and other projects between 1968 and 1970, and they had continued to keep in touch over the years. He was very interested in my work and had on several occasions offered to help us put the NET device on the international market commercially when the time was right. During a visit to Herman in California to discuss developments on the machine, and to get advice on how to proceed once the clinical trials in England were completed, George also went to visit an old friend in the Los Angeles area, Jim Brusseau.

At the time Jim was living aboard a yacht in Marina Del Rey, in the Los Angeles area, with a woman friend, Terri Hurst, and during their conversation George discovered that Terri had been with the Synanon organisation for several years. In fact, she was a founder-member of Synanon. Although she was not, and never had been, a drug addict, her husband, Jack Hurst, had been; and, a few years after they were married, when his addiction was out of control, they had heard of Chuck Dederich and went to Los Angeles to consult with him. It was at the beginning of the Synanon discussions which led to its formation, and her husband Jack, after his cure, stayed on and was the director of the

organisation, while she was the director of the psychotherapeutic techniques used in the Synanon Game.

Naturally, George as a journalist was fascinated with this
first-hand source of information on the mysterious Synanon
organisation, of which so little was known, although its
techniques were being widely copied. He was especially
intrigued as to why she had left the organisation, for she was
obviously impressed by many of its practices, while at the
same time evasive regarding why she had left.

It gradually emerged in conversation that she and her
husband had separated because of the increasingly bizarre
activities of the organisation; later they had left the
organisation for different reasons and they were now in
hiding from the feared Synanon guards. Although Terri
herself had received no direct threats her ex-husband, Jack,
had come home one evening to find his house broken into,
all the lights left blazing, and his guard dog strangled on the
verandah. Nothing had been stolen, so the message to him
was clear: nobody was allowed to leave Synanon without
permission.

Terri had been approached for the story about her
experiences many times by various media journalists but she
had refused them all, except for one who discovered her
whereabouts, and even then she had only confirmed what he
had found out elsewhere and would provide him with
nothing new. She was not only terrified about what might
happen to her, she was also reluctant to have the 'good' of
the Synanon experience distorted by journalists for the sake
of a scoop. She and her husband, as well as many others,
had certainly benefited greatly in the beginning, and she was
bewildered and anguished that something which had been
so good could have gone so wrong. She was still able to
recall the excitement of the discovery of ideas that were
found to work, the sense of fulfilment as thousands of
people were helped to a better life; then the disappointment
as everything they had forged and built deteriorated into
bitterness, coercion and exploitation.

When Terri found that George was able to understand the reasons for the good and the bad she told him that, if he would write about it, she would talk with him about all the details. She was prepared to put her life at risk to get this across. But George, regretfully, told her that he was now occupied with the preparations for our own drug work at Broadhurst Manor, and that he was no longer free to take up journalistic assignments. But he offered to speak with some of his responsible television film producer friends when he returned to England. Terri was dubious, but finally agreed.

George spoke with Adrian Cowell and Norman Stone, but both of them were involved with other projects at the time. However, Norman was interested enough to add it to his list of proposed subjects for filming—if George would do the synopsis. Norman was not too hopeful, for it was widely known that Synanon had sued the powerful Hearst newspaper chain for US$40 million, the ABC-TV network for US$42 million, and *Time* magazine for US$76 million, for just reporting minor incidents about Synanon. So Norman thought it unlikely that the BBC would want to get involved with a project which had such a high risk of litigation.

He was wrong. The BBC were very interested, and wanted him to start on the Synanon story right away. But they, and Norman, wanted George to be part of the film team. As it happened, all of this was taking place in the early months of 1979 while I was in the United States. After I returned to England in May I was told that it was going to take several months to complete the alterations to Broadhurst Manor required by the fire and medical authorities. George was working furiously on the rehabilitation material needed for the clinic when it opened, but doing the Synanon film for the BBC would also provide him with invaluable new insights and information to use in his work at our clinic. So he agreed to go. He was thrilled to be back in television again, and was excited by the challenge of doing another 'impossible' documentary; for, to be successful, he and Norman agreed that he would have to get into one of Synanon's impregnable fortress-like rehabilitation facilities in California.

With one of these 'coincidences' that seemed to occur at crucial points in our lives (a recent example was the meeting with Terri Hurst on Jim's boat), as we were listening to the radio at breakfast one morning, there was an announcement that the Pulitzer Prize for journalism had been awarded to the editor of an obscure small-town newspaper in northern California, Dave Mitchell of the Point Reyes *Light*. It had been awarded to him for his impressive journalistic investigations of Synanon.

The television team now had a launching point for their investigations and they went to Point Reyes (population 300) in Marin County, in northern California. A few miles along the road from Point Reyes was the largest of the Synanon rehabilitation centres. That began a hair-raising time for the television unit as they sought ways to interview and film the Synanon personnel and facilities. They were watched constantly, and on one occasion were chased away by one of the feared 'goon squads'. Eventually George was able to get inside and to interview several of the leading Synanon figures, but they would not allow the interviews to be filmed. What was interesting was that they did not allow George to participate in one of their 'Game' sessions while he was with them, although they had at first agreed to allow him to do so. They never explained why they cancelled the arrangement, but it was significant that it was immediately after he had had an intensive discussion about their methods that they decided 'it would not be appropriate'.

Among the items of information that George had been able to elicit from the reluctant leaders was the admission that Chuck Dederich was not available for any talks, because he had gone back on to alcohol and drugs. Dederich's son wanted his father to submit himself to the rigours of the Synanon Game he had developed, but Dederich's daughter—who had the greater influence in Synanon at this stage—was opposed to the proposal.

When the film was shown to a huge audience in October, 1979, it received excellent notices from the critics. Quite a number of them commented on the material provided by Terri Hurst in her filmed interview. Although there were anonymous threats of 'reprisals' following on the showing of the film, no action against the BBC was ever taken.

Because of the importance of the issues raised by the film we organised a special conference to debate them, at which there were speakers from the United States as well as Britain. We felt that if an eclectic and empirical treatment process such as Synanon could be so successful and acceptable that it was already producing imitators of its earlier practices in the United States and other countries of the world, then a treatment process that had as its foundation the Judaeo-Christian values which had stood the test of several millennia would be even more internationally successful. This was the basis for our own treatment programme in Broadhurst Manor, which was due to open as the 'Pharmakon Clinic' at the beginning of 1980. The word 'Pharmakon' was derived from the Greek *pharmakos*, as described by the theologian-philosopher, Paul Tillich, in his book *The Meaning of Health*:

> The clearest expression of the connection between disease and death, on the one hand, and salvation and eternal life (*not* to be confused with physical immortality), on the other hand, is the famous description of the sacramental food as a *pharmakon athanasias*, a medicine which heals from death, and overcomes exclusion from the realm of eternity . . .

The unique character of the Pharmakon Clinic was in its emphasis on true physiological detoxification and applied spiritual rehabilitation. Synanon's early ambition was to detoxify in the sense of 'drying out' only; and then to attempt to 'purge' the addict of the underlying contributive addiction condition of lies, deceits, hypocrisies and hatreds by 'non-spiritual' emotional confrontations and supportive compassion. Their 'encounter therapy' was an essential part of the treatment of any addict, and although Synanon's method was radical in emphasis it met the fundamental requirements of the condition at that level. One leading authority had written:

> The ordinary psychiatric patient is like a burr, offering many hooks to the world and to the therapist—often too many; the therapist's best strategy is to stand still and let his patient attach himself as he will. But the addict is like a nut: smooth, with a thick armour. The only hook he offers is his need for drugs, and that can be satisfied in a number of ways. To reach the addict, his shell must be cracked. *We might guess that it would be necessary to counter the coercion of opiates with the coercion of therapy.* (my italics)

The same writer said:

> Addicted patients are asocial, inadequate, immature and unstable. They are selfish and self-centred without interest in the welfare of others and are only concerned with their own problems. Their major problem is in the maintenance of their supply of drugs or in the immediate gratification of their desire for drugs. They will resort to any means—however unreasonable or dangerous—to satisfy this insistent craving. They have failed to develop normal human relationships and are almost totally without concern for the distress they inflict on their relatives. They lack self-discipline, willpower or ambition and avoid responsibility. They have a low threshold for pain or any form of discomfort, and are unable to tolerate

criticism or bear frustration. Their personal relationships tend to become restricted to other members of the drug addicts' world, and thus they become social outcasts and very lonely people.

A mutual understanding of this condition, a willingness to confront it as soon as possible in the treatment process, and the ability to provide answers to the complex web of psychospiritual circumstances which are strangling addicts are essential components of any treatment process—in other words, a combination of confrontation and transfor-mation. This is what we aimed for in our Pharmakon Clinic. The addicts were in prison ('addiction' means 'bondage') and they had to be released before they could be properly cured.

The clinic could accommodate twenty patients at a time. Besides myself as senior medical consultant, the medical staff included one other doctor, a nursing supervisor and the equivalent of eleven full-time nurses. George had a number of full-time counsellors on his staff, and we had an administrator, secretary, housekeeper, gardener etc., adding up to a total of twenty-five staff. We lived together with the staff and patients and considered the observable interaction an important part of the therapeutic process.

We were convinced from our experience, as well as from research, that addiction was caused by a lack of meaningful relationships with family, relatives, community and God, and a lack of a meaningful experiential framework to cope with the individual addict's chosen environment. So we treated the whole person—body, mind and spirit—in order to cure both the superficial chemical, and also the behavioural addictions—the workaholism, or addiction to performance; the mammonism, or addiction to making money; the sportaholism, or addiction to excitement; the gambling, or addiction to risk-taking—and the underlying causes which produced the addiction in the first place.

Our counselling was based on the conviction that life held an ultimate meaning, and that this was knowable by any individual who was prepared to seek it out. The goal of the treatment was to provide the individual with a spiritual compass with which to begin a new journey, and to let him or her experience the excitement of being transformed into a new world of which he or she was a meaningful part.

If the *goal* of therapy, however, was to be 'transformation', the *means* was 'confrontation'. This usually began when I first saw the patient and asked them what they were taking, and how much. The usual response, after mentioning the substance of addiction, was probably about half the amount they were really taking (either that or double the amount, if they were the boastful type), because they did not want it to be known what they had to do to pay for the true amount of their particular indulgence. At that stage I always pointed out that I assumed they would be lying to me as they had lied to parents, spouses, employers, and that this had hardened into a practice of lying, deceits and hypocrisies—which would have to be dealt with if they were to be really cured.

Pharmakon Clinic was not a religious organisation. As we had done in the past, we would be treating Moslems, Buddhists, Marxists and Hindus, as well as Christians, agnostics and atheists who needed freedom from chemical and behavioural addictions. But it would be staffed preferably, if such people became available, by personnel who had a wholesome commitment to Judaeo-Christian ideals as well their professional expertise. There would be no psychiatrists on the resident or consultant staff, since we believed addiction to be fundamentally a spiritual problem requiring spiritual solutions—which could be more adequately provided by trained paraprofessionals with a knowledge and experience of addictions and spiritual values.

At Pharmakon the addicts would be taught that, to remain free from drugs, an individual had to become God-centred instead of self-centred, God-controlled instead of self-directed. For it is self-interest which is the bondage of the addict. The addict is not just in bondage to the demands of the chemical substance, as was demonstrated by detoxification from its effects. The true bondage was the addiction to a lifestyle of impotence—even at the price of its accompanying self-loathing. It was not just the drug-free life which was empty; it was also the inner self. It was not just the drug-free life which was without meaning; it was the inner self which was devoid of values.

A person had to have a belief if he or she was to have values—a belief that was more than a mere mental assent to a set of theological propositions. A value could be defined as: a belief freely chosen from among alternatives, after careful consideration of the consequences of each alternative; a belief that was prized, so that the person was happy with the choice; a belief that was important enough for a person to publicly affirm the choice; a belief that was acted on repeatedly, over a period of time, and incorporated into a person's behaviour.

When we did eventually get the clinic operating we had used up so much of our donation from the Rank Foundation in training staff, furnishing the rooms and buying necessary equipment, that we only had enough to last us for the first three months of operation, unless we could find other sources of income. We were admitting twenty-five per cent of patients who were too poor to pay, and we were meeting their expenses out of our charity FREE!. But with George involved in the day-to-day counselling in the clinic he was no longer able to find time to go out fund-raising. Also, most people who had been interested in my work thought we had already left Britain, because of the BBC film which had showed us packing to go to the United States in 1977.

The perilous state of our finances precipitated a crisis in our staff relations. We had become aware that the endless bureaucratic delays, and the multiplying problems of a new work being established, were affecting some of the staff more than others. Some of them saw the difficulties as a challenge and were glad to attempt to overcome them, but some felt their security was at stake and sought to have the remaining money paid to them as compensation while they looked for new jobs. When their attempts at persuading others to join them failed, they tried the strong-arm tactics of threatening to resign *en bloc*.

Unhappily all those taking this action were professing Christians and their reasons ranged through the following:

- It was 'not God's will'.
- George was introducing 'Synanon techniques'.
- Finance was inadequate.
- It was 'bad Christian stewardship' to open without sufficient money.
- My treatment was 'dangerous' (without any attempt at proof or explanation).

Fortunately, when they took the matter to the Rank Foundation they were given short shrift, and told that the Rank Trustees had full confidence in George and me. The 'core group', as they called themselves during the dispute, were shattered when their resignations were accepted, with immediate effect, and they were asked to leave the clinic within twenty-four hours.

One of the benefits to emerge from the crisis in the clinic was the assurance from the Marie Curie Laboratories that their findings demonstrated the claims of the so-called 'core group' about NET being 'dangerous' to be nonsense. In fact, the research at the laboratories was producing new and exciting possibilities. They had begun to investigate the effects of NET in alcoholism and liver conditions, and in the process were discovering significant developments in the amelioration of stress. They could establish beyond doubt that the pulse frequency of the electrical stimulus was an important factor, and that certain specific frequencies were affecting specific conditions. This was very satisfying to me, for I had been noting just such reactions from my own clinical observations.

We had opened the clinic with only six patients in order to give the new nursing staff time and opportunity to become accustomed to the NET treatment process, and to get the nurses and the counsellors in their different activities into an effective working pattern.

By March—the critical third month when we were supposed to close because of lack of money—we had enough money to keep us going for another two months, and we were now equipped to take in more patients. We had agreed with the loyal staff who had remained with us during and after the crisis that whatever happened we would give them early warning of possible closure and one month's notice with pay.

Already we were finding unexpected but exciting developments from our model clinic. The most important was the apparent acceleration of benefits experienced by the patients in this 'group' setting, compared with what I had known when only treating single patients individually. In the clinic, as they arrived, they could see for themselves the earlier patients who were as badly, or worse, addicted than they were; yet, after only a few days—when from their previous experience they knew they should be at their worst—they saw them looking well and working around the clinic without any drugs whatever.

Then the clinic itself, in its incomparable setting, provided beauty and tranquillity, recreational and work therapy, in a residential rather than an institutional form. Our patients were from all classes, from the prostitute daughter of a prostitute mother hooked on a variety of drugs and alcohol, to a member of one of the highest families in the land suffering from chronic pain (I felt the ethos of the clinic was established when the daily rota of activities brought them both together to do the washing-up, and they later confessed to being deeply impressed by each other's experiences!). The whole atmosphere was serene, cheerful, positive and optimistic, and exceeding all my expectations.

Many relatives, and girlfriends in particular, were

astonished that there was never any violence in the clinic, because in their experience the addicts were often violent at home, either when in need of drugs or when threatening to get money for their drugs. Actually, there were two occasions when violence seemed imminent.

Because George and I lived on the premises we were called in whenever any crisis arose—from fixing electrical fuses to patient problems—day and night, seven days a week. Saturday and Sunday were especially busy, because that was the time when most parents or spouses wished to visit, and always wanted to talk with George and me because the regular counsellors were off duty at the weekends. I also had to check all the detailed data-recording, answer correspondence, and take the nonstop phonecalls because the clerical staff were also off-duty.

Because of these more than demanding circumstances on one occasion George and I were grateful for an opportunity to celebrate our first weekend off in several months, and we left for London on the Saturday afternoon. We had just sat down with a gathering of friends at Norman Stone's flat when a phonecall came from the counsellor who was standing in for George. There had been an altercation when one of the men patients found that his girlfriend had been having an affair with another patient in the clinic, and was going to leave him and go off with the new lover. The rejected boyfriend had gone into the kitchen and got a sharp knife and was threatening to kill his rival. Normally, we never allowed couples to be admitted together for treatment at the same time, but the spurned lover had arrived just before his girlfriend was due to leave.

We left London and drove madly back to the clinic, not knowing what to expect when we arrived. As it happened, the rejected lover had only stuck his knife into a chair in his rage, and had been calmed down somewhat. After George and I had a straight talk with him, and with the other two involved, everything quietened down. But it meant that our 'quiet' weekend was irretrievably ruined.

The other occasion of potential violence involved a patient whom I shall call Paddy—although that was not his real name. Paddy was a red-headed alcoholic Catholic, with a long record of violence when he was brought to our clinic by the family priest. Even when he was sober, Paddy was a menacing figure, surly, brooding and given to unpredictable rages. The patients and staff were all edgy around him. He did little to mitigate this impression, and was sullen, vituperatively complaining, and uncooperative.

In the clinic it was the normal practice, after the first few days when possible physical and psychological distress were being eased by the NET treatment, that all patients attend the morning meditation period. This was when George set the theme for the day's individual and group discussions by taking an excerpt from the Bible, or some other book, and after explaining its meaning opened the session up for the general participation of the patients.

Paddy came late the first morning he was due to attend, then did not appear the following morning at all. George enquired of the doctor and nurses if he was all right and fit to attend, and they confirmed that he was. A few of the staff, however, indicated that he had either stayed in bed, or was lounging around somewhere, and they were too afraid to make an issue of it with him. George told them that he wanted a full report about Paddy's movements next morning, before meditation began.

The following morning the staff told George that Paddy was still in bed and had not even come down for breakfast. George went to his room and asked him to get up to attend morning meditation. He told George, cursing, what he could do with both himself and meditation. George told him quietly but firmly that if he did not get up right away he would make sure he did. Paddy cursed him even more, and turned his face away. George yanked off the bedclothes with one pull, and Paddy grabbed at his suddenly exposed private parts, yelling threats. George told him calmly that he was going for a basin of cold water next, and Paddy jumped out of bed and made for him until they stood nose to nose. George laconically warned Paddy to take care, that his groin was only inches from his knee, and Paddy jumped back.

'You have a choice,' George informed him neutrally. 'You can put on your clothes and come to meditation right away; or you can put on your clothes, pack your bag and leave the clinic.' George turned away and left the room. Paddy appeared at meditation shortly afterwards.

Some time later we sent for him to see us in the study, and we talked quietly. After asking George interestedly if he would really have kneed him in the groin, and being told by George cheerfully that he would, had it been necessary, Paddy told us that he didn't know his father, his mother had spoiled him outrageously, his wife was a church-going teetotaller with a domineering and interfering mother, and so on. He had found as a child that he could get his way by being threatening, whether inside or outside the home, and as an adult this had become a way of life for him. He was genuinely fond of his wife, but found it impossible to communicate with her because of her dependence on her mother, and her passion for her mother's approval above his own.

We sent for his wife to come to the clinic and, after reprimanding her for her unhealthy subservient relationship with her mother, persuaded her to be more considerate of Paddy's problems. We suggested that they both sit down and work at trying to communicate reasonably with each other. We proposed that she go with him to the pub, if he agreed to take only the one or two drinks he insisted was all he ever wanted; she need not take more than a soft drink. We persuaded him to take the two drinks at most, because of his wife's justifiable fear of his excessive drinking. Paddy was to curb his acquired tendency of trying to get his own way by using violence or threats of violence.

(Almost a year later, we were driving through a town in the north of England where Paddy lived. We did not have his address, but we did have the address of the family priest and we called on him. He told us with delight that Paddy was a changed man, with no alcohol problems at all. With the priest's help Paddy and his wife had sold their home and had bought another larger place, which both of them had renovated and furnished as a halfway house for recovering alcoholics and drug addicts.)

By the autumn we were up to almost full occupancy of twenty patients, and very close to financial viability. We now felt confident enough to organise a national medical conference, and to invite international authorities in the drug addiction and electrical stimulation field to participate. I was thrilled when the prestigious Royal Society of Medicine approved my request to hold the first Neuro-Electric Therapy Conference in their premises in Central London. This elation increased when several of the world's leading authorities on electrical stimulation accepted my invitation to participate.

The speakers' panel included Dr Robert Becker, the pioneer in regenerating bone tissue by electrostimulation in cases of nonunion, who had been so helpful to me over the years in my own research and treatment; Dr Irving Cooper, the pioneer of cryogenic surgery, who was now implanting electrodes in the brain for the treatment of epileptics and spastics; Dr John Hughes, the co-discoverer with Dr Hans Kosterlitz, of enkephalin; Dr John Liebeskind, an international authority on the endogenous mechanisms of pain inhibition, and its control in animals by electrical stimulation of the brain; Dr Leon Illis and Dr John Bates, well-known for their work in electrostimulation in the treatment of multiple sclerosis and chronic pain.

The clinic had demonstrated that the NET treatment, together with our own version of psychospiritual rehabilitation based on Judaeo-Christian values, was likely to be very successful. We had been visited by an impressive number of medical and social representatives from several countries, in addition to the many from different parts of the United Kingdom, who wanted to know when the NET stimulators and our counselling material would be available for them to use. But our very success had highlighted a weakness: my most recent NET Model IV designed for use in the clinical trial, although the most advanced, was also the most complicated, and required from three to six months for our nurses to learn how to operate the complex variety of frequencies in the treatment of various forms of addiction. It was obvious to me, therefore, that the device would have to be miniaturised and computerised so that it could be used more simply by medical and para-medical personnel. This would eliminate the need for lengthy, expensive and time-consuming tutorials.

In November 1980 we had eighteen patients, and the clinic had reached financial viability as a self-operating unit. The Rank Foundation agreed to let us have the use of Broadhurst Manor at a peppercorn rent for five years. Because it was the end of the year, with Christmas and New Year holidays approaching, and our loyal and enthusiastic staff had taken no holidays but were required to take them under their union regulations, we were faced with the urgent need for another £30,000 as bridging finance with which to start up in the coming New Year for the first three months.

November was our crisis month, too, in that we had agreed to give the staff one month's notice if we were not going to be able to continue; so, if we did not have the £30,000 in hand in November we were bound by our promise to let the staff know and go before the holidays. Everyone tried everything they knew to raise the money. We even wrote to the Prime Minister, Margaret Thatcher, pleading for special consideration in view of the seriousness of the drug problem and the contribution we could make to a solution. All to no avail.

Pete Townshend and Eric Clapton performed two rock music concerts on our behalf at the Rainbow Theatre, to raise £20,000; but the money would not be available for a few months into the New Year, and the bank would not accept the risk to let us have a bridging loan.

Ironically, the BBC had approached us again about doing a third film documentary in a series entitled *Open Secret*—this time with Peter Williams as producer, and not our friend, Norman Stone—to explore the scientific rather than the human interest aspect of my work. They filmed in the clinic itself, and in the Marie Curie Laboratories where they interviewed the scientist doing the laboratory work on NET (who admitted on camera that he had not believed in the NET theories when he had begun the research in 1979, but had observed the positive response on animals under investigation), and finally a variety of doctors both for and against my work. The film, entitled *The Black Box*, was shown to a great deal of favourable reaction in February 1981, the month after the clinic officially closed.

'The Black Box' (MEGANET Model IV) as shown on the BBC film, with Meg demonstrating the controls. 1980

I was inconsolable, as were the staff. They, with me, had tried so hard, given so much, been so deeply involved in the challenges and responses, had been so uplifted and excited by the new personal dimension in healing broken lives as well as sick minds and bodies, and had come so close to realising the long-fought-for dream of launching this pioneering venture on a desperately sick nation and world, that its sudden ending left us all shattered and numb.

Only George was composed in the face of the disaster. He had been saying for the past few months that we might have to face this possibility, and that it could be a good thing in that it would, among other things, release me to apply myself to the developing of a new, more advanced and easier-to-use model of my NET stimulator which could be used by everybody. With that new model available it would then be possible to tackle the drug problem in a more comprehensive manner, when all doctors and clinics and hospitals could use it, instead of us having to establish and organise individual clinics. We had learned enough in the past year of the clinical trial to produce a drug treatment paradigm which could be introduced rapidly throughout the world.

I was not wholly comforted, but it helped. As with all our decisions affecting the family, we talked over the situation and its consequences together. Lorne, now twenty-one years old, was due to complete the psychiatric nursing training that he had taken up in order to help me with the practical aspects of the NET treatment. Sean, at nineteen, had changed his earlier ambition to study astrophysics to chemistry and biochemistry to help me with the scientific rationale of NeuroElectric Therapy. Myrrh, at seventeen, was still undecided but thought she might study medicine or nursing, also to help with the treatment. It was very satisfying to both George and me to have their confidence in this way, after they had been called on to sacrifice so much in their childhood and adolescence, while we battled on to realise a dream—or, rather, fulfil a vision.

George and I had become increasingly conscious over the years of the need to handle our own family problems well if we were going to be in the position of advising others. We had spent a great part of our lives abroad among families—diplomats' families, business families, professional families, missionary families—where the children were sacrificed to the demands of the parents' jobs and lifestyles. So we had made it a practice to include them in our decisions from an early age.

Now, faced with the prospects of no employment again, no home, no income, no insurance even—for all had gone to help the NET work forward—it would mean the scattering of the family once more among friends willing to take them, deprivation of several kinds, and possibly several years of hardship all round.

'When was it ever anything else?' Lorne asked rhetorically. 'It's not a new situation. We'll survive this, too.'

The others agreed. With our family relationship still intact in the face of the overwhelming problems, I felt able to face the uncertain future again.

We began the depressing task of dismantling the clinic, and packing our goods for storage yet again. We had no place to put our things, and could not afford storage charges, but George's brother, Bill, offered to take what he could in his basement, and his sister, Margaret, took the remainder into a garden shed, in their homes in Scotland. We had to stay on in London because there was a monumental amount of work to be done in collating all the findings of the past year, and keeping them available for statistical analysis and publication.

A good friend, Trish Williams, offered us the use of a bedroom in her home while we got ourselves organised. Lorne was being housed at the hospital. Sean went to live with Norman and some of his friends for a time, sleeping on the floor of the crowded apartment, and then found a flat in south London; it meant a sixteen-mile bicycle ride to and from the Imperial College of Science in London University every day, rain, sleet, snow or shine, but he faced it cheerfully. Myrrh went to live with another friend, Elizabeth Aitken.

All my filing cabinets and tea-chests of research notes were put in storage, and we had two suitcases of personal effects left between us. I had memories of 1954 in Kalimpong; 1963 in London; 1964 in Kathmandu; 1971 in Hong Kong; 1974 in London—no money, no home, no immediate prospects.

It was now February, 1981, and we had nothing with which to face the future. Most people at our ages were considering retirement, and here we were still looking for a way to change the world. What was it Jesus said? 'A person's life does not consist in the abundance of things possessed . . . For where your treasure is, there will your heart be also.'

After thirty years we still had each other, we had a loving family, we had a glorious vision spread before us. We had treasure beyond price.

- 10 -
Starting Again in the USA

While I began the dispiriting round of visits to organisations and individuals seeking finance to carry on my work, George wrote letters requesting the same. I even offered my services to the government to be used in any capacity, anywhere, to further the treatment of drug and alcohol addictions—but they wrote to say that only local authorities in each Health Area could make appointments.

Then George had a letter from his eighty-year-old financier friend in California, Herman Kingsley:

'. . . If we can get together, and you don't want too much, I have people who are ready to build a plant large enough to build the machine at the right price. I have lined up the top men in the country who know how to manufacture, merchandise, and have enough money to go nationally . . . we are talking of millions. As you know, I do not want to do something unless it is worthwhile. I have a company that will take a minimum of 5000 machines each time, and that's a drop in the bucket . . . This is big, and all that is needed is enough money in one country to put it world-wide . . . Speed is important! Money does not wait for anyone! . . .'

Once again we had to scrape around in order to find the money for our air fares to take us to the United States. We had an invitation from the pastor of a small church in Point Reyes, in northern California, whom George had met while they were doing the Synanon film, to come and live with them, and they would provide food and lodging for us. We went there while we had discussions with Herman.

The millionaires who were interested, he said, wanted to have a watertight arrangement regarding patent and other commercial considerations. If we were envisaging a medical breakthrough on a large scale, with associated million- or even billion-dollar profits, then industrial espionage had to be taken seriously. So, there would have to be no publicity, no lectures at medical conferences, until everything was secured.

In order to make certain that there could be no objections to patent from my public lectures and writings from the past, he insisted that I would have to have an altogether new machine which would include new material. I told him about my proposals for an advanced model which could be operated more simply but which required a high degree of technological expertise. He said that he himself had three engineering degrees, and that he would get the help of a former chairman of a large nuclear engineering enterprise, who was now retired, to help me with my new model.

But when I had discussions with them, I found their tendency was to oversimplify the requirements to suit their own experience in the past. It was very difficult for engineering and electronics experts to accept that there were biochemical factors outside their range of experience which were of great importance in the skilled delivery of the signals that I needed to effect cures. It was so much easier to pat me metaphorically on the head and imply, 'Don't you worry your pretty little head; just leave this to us men who are used to solving problems in a man's world'—an attitude I had never once experienced in my surgical career.

As the months passed, and they had still not come up with a machine that came near to my specifications, it looked as if we had reached a dead end. If I could not get the technology that I needed to develop my machine in Silicon Valley, then I was not going to get it anywhere.

During one of our discussions the pastor of the church in Point Reyes (with less than thirty members) said that there was an elder in the church who was something of an expert in electronics; perhaps he could help? It was a bizarre suggestion in the circumstances. I had discussed my requirements with the best experts in Britain, and with the supposed best experts in California, and they had come up with nothing. What could the local electrician from a small township offer?

However, the pastor called in his young church elder, Walter Underhill, for a talk after supper, and I tried to describe what it was that I wanted. I had scarcely started when Walter began to ask the right questions and before long was making tentative suggestions. I could not believe what I was hearing, for Walter was so diffident with his ideas that I thought he had not adequately grasped what I needed. But, eventually, after he had scribbled an outline of what he was proposing on some scrap sheets of paper, I asked if he could come up with a working model. He said confidently that he could—'if I had the time and money.' Like so many of the modern Silicon Valley entrepreneurs, Walter had been playing and working with electronics since he was a few years old, and although he had no university degree in the subject he had had in-depth training and experience, and was extremely skilful.

Initially, Herman laughed off my proposal, but neither he nor his retired expert could provide answers, and it was agreed that Walter should go ahead. He worked on a 'breadboard' model in his small wooden workshop at the foot of his garden, and, with his own 'hobby' oscilloscope and computer, worked out the technical solutions. Fortunately our son, Sean, was on holiday from his studies at the Imperial College of Science and he was able to come out to California and work with Walter.

When Walter had completed the 'breadboard' to his satisfaction, and he and Sean had demonstrated to me on the oscilloscope that it did what I wanted, we were ready to proceed. But, once again we were delayed as Herman haggled with financiers over participation in any proposed corporation to exploit the machine's potential. There was no shortage of either money or interest, for 'biotechnology' was now the 'in' market in Wall Street and billions had been being poured into genetic engineering. When the new genetic engineering corporations were still not producing anything that was marketable, there were plenty of people with available money ready to invest in my machine.

Walter Underhill (left) and Sean working on what proved to be the earliest stage of our Research Model VII of the MEGANET, in a shed in Walter's garden in Point Reyes, Marin County.
1981

This was amusing, as we were now at yet another low ebb in our living situation. We had been sleeping on two camp beds in the small church vestry, and eating food supplied from the few church members, while we were developing the new machine. Then, when the information about the commercial possibilities began to circulate, the pastor and the church began to lose sight of the spiritual vision and think of the material prospects. When the pastor announced that the next prayer and Bible study meeting would be a discussion on what kind of cars and houses the members could expect from the profits of the machines, we decided that matters had gone too far and warned them that it might take years before there was that kind of money; and, anyway, it was the spiritual and not the material potential which should be occupying their attention.

The pastor was angry enough to ask us to leave the vestry and church, and we were without a place to stay again. However, by one of these strange provisions which God used to save us from total disaster, we had been given the keys of a second house belonging to a former American drug addict whom we had successfully treated at Broadhurst Manor, in case we ever needed a place, and it was only a few miles away at San Rafael. But when Walter offered to take us there in his van, the pastor, in his frustration and disappointment at not being made wealthy, threw Walter and his family out of the church and from their home in the church grounds.

Some other Christian friends, Louis and Mary Neely, from a church in Sacramento, to the north of San Rafael, gave us the use of a van, and enough money to keep us in food. What was even more interesting was that one of their elders, Herb Ellingwood, who had a particular interest in drug and alcohol work, was now in Washington DC where he was Deputy Legal Counsel to President Reagan in the White House. Louis and Mary wrote to him to let him know about the NET treatment, and asked him to arrange a meeting with anybody influential who might help the work forward.

We had now been in the United States for over six months with little to show for it, and our children were having to battle with their own problems in London without our help. I had just said to George that at least we should be thankful we had our health when I had a bad attack of influenza, which left me with a distressing conjunctivitis.

I still had not got over this when George developed a sudden pain in his neck and shoulders, which quickly became so crippling that he was immobilised on the downstairs couch, in one position, unable to write, or even read for more than a few minutes. He had been writing steadily for months—even for the past few years, as he prepared all the material that we would need for counselling in the future—and this concentrated activity, mostly by pen rather than typewriter, had resulted in the sudden onset of a characteristic pinched nerve. The fingers of his right hand were also affected so that he could no longer hold a pen, or type. It also meant that he could not shop, or cook, or drive the van. I had a history of back trouble and had to be careful what I lifted, the heavy van was difficult for me to drive, and I could not carry the bags of shopping, so that between us we were now almost completely incapacitated.

While we were at our new low ebb, the mail brought a letter from a friend whom George had known several years before, when he had visited the United States, Luci Shaw. She and her husband had a publishing company in Wheaton, Illinois, and Luci herself was a well-known poet whose writings George greatly appreciated. She was writing to him now because she had just read an article in which he was being interviewed and she wanted to know if he was interested in writing a book for them, or if I would, about my work.

In her letter she enclosed a card printed with one of her recent poems, entitled *The Foolishness of God*:

Perform impossibilities
or perish. Thrust out now
the unseasonal ripe figs
among your leaves. Expect
the mountain to be moved.
Hate parents, friends and all
materiality. Love every enemy.
Forgive more times than seventy-
seven. Camel-like, squeeze by
into the kingdom through
the needle's eye. All fear quell.
Hack off your hand, or else,
unbloodied, go to hell.

Thus the divine unreason.
Despairing now, you cry
with earthy logic—*How*?
and I, your God, reply:
Leap from your weedy shallows.
Dive into the moving water.
Eyeless, learn to see
truly. Find in my folly your
true sanity. Then, Spirit-driven,
run on my narrow way, sure
as a child. Probe, hold
my unhealed hand, and
bloody, enter heaven.

George had looked at it for so long I asked what he was
reading, and he handed the card to me. I read it all, and
handed it back. In the conversation that followed George
told me he had been lying there on the couch for the past
few weeks, trying to work out how we could proceed with
the project with him confined indefinitely to a wheelchair to
support his neck. The only alternative left to us, it seemed,
was to drop the project here in the United States, and to
return to England—where there was minimum interest. We
were looking at the end of the vision.

It was at this point the letter, and the card, arrived, like
a tocsin sounding down through the years: 'Perform impossibilities or perish . . .' Even the title of the poem, *The Foolishness of God*, was reminiscent, for George's second book
had been entitled *God's Fool*, and it had been taken from a
poem of that name. The first stanza of that poem had read:

Let me stand with the conquered who assayed
A greater thing than sane men can imagine
Or pious hearts believe. Some love of Death
Seized all their being and hurl'd them against the
        World;
And mocking all intelligence they fell . . .

George dictated a reply for me to send to Luci saying that he would be in touch with her fairly soon regarding a book of some kind. Meanwhile, he began making notes on a series of books on the theme of *The Impossible God*, a record of God's dealings with His creatures from the beginning, and His eternal purposes for them, which would comprise altogether a 'Journalist's Bible'. It would form the capstone of his own life's experience.

I put George on my NET stimulator and experimented with a variety of frequencies. He had been X-rayed and we had seen that the nerve was pinched between the sixth and seventh vertebrae. This helped me to understand some more uses of the machine, and also helped in modifying his pain when he moved. We had no other alternatives, for we had no money to pay for the services of a doctor in America, or for a hospital visit.

At this point Herman arranged for us to go to southern California to live with a Dr William 'Cherry' Parker. Dr Parker was in charge of a holistic clinic in Newport Beach, and Herman had an arrangement with him to use the new machine in trials there. I was concerned about the close association with the holistic movement, which was known for many bizarre practices, cultic theories, Eastern mysticism and psychic healers, but I had little choice in the matter. I needed money. I needed machines. I needed results to evaluate. At the end of the day it would be my results which counted, not any bizarre or sensational circumstances with which they might be surrounded.

After all, what could be more bizarre than our present circumstances? In addition to the personal and domestic problems, I was shut away from all contact with professional colleagues, not permitted to write or research or lecture at a critical stage of pioneering discovery; while multimillion-dollar negotiations were being conducted in my name, multinational operations being planned, and mind-boggling figures being tossed around. Somewhere in these labyrinthine complexities there was a design, a purpose, for

George and me and for our children—occasionally comprehended, often glimpsed, sometimes stumbled over, periodically resented, but ultimately accepted as a necessary way to go. As Isaiah the Prophet said: 'The lame shall take the prey.'

We had to return the van to our church friends in Sacramento but our former missionary friends, Vik and Helen Hjelmervik, lived in Los Angeles and Vik said we could have one of his family vehicles. The Sacramento church arranged for one of the members to come and collect their van after we reached Los Angeles. George was still not able to drive, I was hardly able to move the gear lever because it was so stiff, but we drove the three hundred miles from San Rafael to Los Angeles, left the Sacramento church van and took Vik's van on to Newport Beach. (Although George was almost completely immobilised for a period of several weeks, he only required a total of six aspirins throughout because the NET kept his pain at a bearable level.)

'Cherry' Parker gave us a warm welcome into his home, and he was a considerate and delightful host. Unfortunately, when Herman and his 'expert' friend brought the new machine which Walter had designed for them it did not work. I suspected that might happen when they did not consult either with me or with Walter during its manufacture. They set up an oscilloscope to demonstrate how it worked perfectly; but when I applied it to myself, or to George, it was useless. They had not taken into consideration the fact that the body itself is a capacitor and materially altered the delivery of currents and wave-forms. The machine, after almost a year, was of no use at all. It was now 1982; it meant starting all over again, I said, and this time I would have to be involved in its development whatever the chauvinistic electronics experts might say.

In the midst of all this embarrassment and confusion I had an urgent telephone call from England. It was from Bill Curbishley, the manager of the rock music group 'The Who', to say that Pete Townshend had been taken to the hospital with an overdose of drugs, and had almost died there. (He has since spoken about this for publication so I can talk about it here.) His stomach had been pumped out but he needed treatment desperately. Could I help? This was followed by an appeal for help from Pete's personal assistant, Judy, who said he had been taking lots of drugs and alcohol recently, and his personal as well as professional life was in a mess. Could they send him to me in California?

I knew that if Pete were as bad as they said, it would be of no use sending an employee to escort him to the United States. When drug addicts were as far gone as Pete was, they were almost unmanageable, willing to promise anything and agree to anything, but as soon as they had an opportunity to break away for drugs they would leave anyone—at home, hospital, or airport. But Lorne had just completed his postgraduate psychiatric nursing studies, and I arranged with him to go and escort Pete personally to the United States, and to help with his treatment.

With Bill Curbishley's approval I rented a small flat near us for Pete and Lorne, so Lorne could supervise the treatment day and night—a very demanding task, with no one to relieve him, but I knew that Pete and Lorne got on well together. I also arranged with a local doctor to supervise and monitor the treatment to conform with American regulations, as I had done with Keith Richards. There was no danger in treating him in a domestic setting since he was only on heroin and cocaine, and people do not die from *stopping* these drugs. Herman was not very happy at the possibility of publicity if the news of Pete's treatment got out to the media, but Pete had been such a good friend to me, and he had done so much to help others when they were in need, that I was prepared to take any risk to help him when he was in trouble.

On the night of his arrival in Los Angeles George and I drove in Vik's old van to the airport. I knew it was unlikely that Pete would risk taking drugs with him on to the plane, so he would probably be in a state of acute withdrawal when he arrived. I took an NET stimulator with me, and I could see from his agitated appearance that he was desperately ill and craving as he came out of the customs area, so I hooked him up to the machine right away. I was horrified to discover that he was also hooked on Ativan, a tranquilliser which could well cause convulsions when it was stopped. But it was late at night and not possible to change arrangements. We had two hours' drive to the flat and before we reached there he had demonstrably calmed down.

Pete made a remarkable recovery considering how far gone he had been, both in London and when he arrived in Los Angeles. Again, it was not enough simply to detoxify from his drugs of addiction, for his return to drugs had been caused by a variety of problems which had to be sorted out to effect a real cure. Some of these were begun while he was in Los Angeles, such as the agreement of his wife to help him by trying to make their broken marriage work again, and the sorting out of his complex business affairs. He himself described his treatment at this time to an interviewer:

> As a matter of fact I got very, very minor withdrawals for the first few days afterwards. But my mood was basically stabilised by the last three days of treatment. Also, I did a lot of exercise and that was a big help . . . By about the third week people who had seen me taking brisk walks would come up to me on the street and say, 'That's California for you. When you first arrived you looked like a corpse. We gave you half an hour to live. And now look at you. All you needed was a few days in California . . .'
>
> Something else happens during Meg's treatment—I mean emotionally. When you first start to recover you feel superhuman. You get swept away by the euphoria of the natural high and the feeling of being able to handle any crisis. But this is where I think

Meg is so clever. It seems she understood that, and in the month I stayed with her she helped me to sublimate that and balance it—in other words, not to overreact, and thus swing the pendulum too far in the other direction. She constantly stressed the spiritual rebuilding I had to do, which I'm *still* dealing with: the importance of getting closer to my children again, and if it was possible—and at the time it didn't look like too hot a situation—to re-establish my relationship with my wife . . .

Meg with Pete Townshend, after his treatment.
1982

While Pete was convalescing in Newport Beach with us he met with former friends he had known in California, and was also entertained by Cherry Parker and others we had come to know. Among these were Ben and Lauretta Patterson, and Bert and Edna Rowe. Ben was the pastor of the Irvine Presbyterian Church, and he and Lauretta were real soul-mates with us and of great help to us spiritually at this time. As Ben had been a founder-editor of the Christian satirical magazine, *The Wittenberg Door*, he and George had a similar sense of humour as well being compatible spiritually. Ben had been a great admirer of 'The Who' and it was a great experience for Pete and Ben and Lauretta to meet.

Bert and Edna we had met when Bert came to visit us as a 'good neighbour'. We discovered that he and Edna were from London, had been in India, and were now resident in California. When Cherry Parker moved away from the area Bert and Edna provided us with an apartment beneath their own, and we became very friendly with them.

My treatment of Pete was not made immediately public but he did not hide himself away as he visited his own former friends. When it became known he had been treated by me, and that I was in the area, I was again pursued by many well-known figures. A group in northern California composed of 'Jefferson Airplane', and 'The Grateful Dead', and other leading people in the rock music and entertainment world, asked me to treat Dave Crosby of 'Crosby, Stills and Nash' as he was in a very bad way. They said he had run through two million dollars because of his drug habit, and as his friends they were trying to put pressure on him to have treatment. I agreed to provide this, but they could not persuade him to make the decision.

One famous person I did treat at that time did not wish it to be known, and again it had to be handled with a great deal of secrecy. The treatment was so successful that the individual concerned donated the money for me to complete the statistical analysis of all the people I had treated over the past eight years, including the clinical trial at Broadhurst Manor. With this money I was able to obtain the services of a qualified statistician, and the approval of the University of California to use its computers.

This came at a very crucial time, for our visas had expired and I was having to obtain a special 'H1' research visa, and this meant that we would have to leave the country. I planned to collect the visa at the United States Embassy in Vancouver, where I had two cousins; but it meant that George would have to return to the United Kingdom until my visa was approved and then apply to join me.

I arranged for George to see a specialist in Scotland about his neck, which was still painful; but advised him not to have an operation, if that was what was advised, until I had seen the surgeon's report. I was aware that the success rate of such an operation was only fifty per cent. Eventually the NET alone was sufficient to cure both the pain and the immobility.

George would also be able to see Sean, now studying at the Imperial College of Science of London University, while he was home, but Myrrh was on an approved sabbatical to the Far East—which she had earned with her own money from operating a sandwich-bar at a leading London establishment. She had gone to India first, to visit people who had known us, including 'Uncle Tenzing' of Mount Everest fame and Dr Pemba, my Tibetan assistant of our Darjeeling days. She then moved on to Hong Kong, where she acted as nanny to two small children whose mother had left them, to support herself until she returned to England to renew her studies. She was eighteen at the time, and travelling on her own. I had not worried when Lorne and Sean went off on their sabbaticals, but I had been petrified at the thought of my young daughter being on her own. I knew of several instances of attacks, rapes, and even one murder of a friend, in India, and these were all older people. When I had argued with George, he said we had to treat Myrrh the same as the two boys, and that he would instruct her how to deal with rapists and thugs!

We had agreed with the children that they could all have one year's sabbatical after they finished school and before they continued with their studies; but they would have to finance that year out of their own earnings. The usual complaint of the young was that, because of the demands of education, they had no chance to experience 'what life is all about'. We told our children that life was all about struggle and challenge and excitement—but that every individual had to find their own place and pay their own price. Lorne had chosen to go to Israel, Europe and America; Sean had chosen to go to Germany, and work in a publisher's firm while learning the language; Myrrh had chosen to visit Asia. She had a wonderful time and arrived home safely. She wrote to us that for the first time she realised the value of her own strict upbringing, when she had to take almost full responsibility for two spoiled, unhappy children. She saw how beautifully they responded to discipline combined with caring, and it almost broke her heart, and theirs, when she had to leave them to start university in London.

While George was still preparing to leave the United States he had a call from his brother, Bill, to say that their mother was critically ill, and was not expected to live. George made arrangements to fly home immediately, but a few hours before he was due to leave, Bill telephoned again to say their mother had died. George left anyway, to attend the funeral.

Lorne and I remained in California, living on twenty-five dollars a week between us, and only going out once a week to buy the groceries. Herman Kingsley, who boasted that he never paid out any of his money in any of his financial ventures, was reluctant to pay even the small amount asked by Edna and Bert Rowe for the rent of their apartment. I had to literally beg him for the money, a humiliating (not humbling!) experience, and on one occasion he said irritably, 'It won't do you any harm to starve.' His grasping personal attitude as he acted for us, with our agreed power of attorney, exasperated the many financiers who were willing to put money into a venture, but who were not prepared to do so blindly without adequate information as Herman was intractably demanding.

I had arranged with George that, when he was at home, he would open up our boxes in storage with Bill and Margaret in Scotland, and get out all the papers of the research notes we had accumulated over the years, so that I could push ahead with my statistical analysis while I was waiting for my new model of the machine to be ready.

When the 'H1 Visa' came through, I had to go to the Vancouver embassy to collect it, and George joined me there. He brought all the case notes of the patients I had treated over the previous seven years. With the visa problem out of the way I was able to move ahead quickly with my statistician associate, Jim Lehman of the University of California, Los Angeles, and we collated the analyses of treatment notes and follow-up questionnaires for my presentation to the British Medical Association, under the requirements of the Doris Odlum award which I had been granted.

Because of the delay in getting my new machine I was also able to prepare three articles for publication in periodicals, and complete the draft of my book, *Getting Off the Hook*, to be published by Harold and Luci Shaw.

- 11 -

Battling Prejudice and Greed in the Commercial Jungle

I received word from Herb Ellingwood, the Christian elder of the church in Sacramento which had been so helpful to us, to say that he would be happy to meet with us at the White House and do what he could to introduce us to the people who were dealing with the drug problem.

Soon afterwards we arranged a visit to Washington and Herb set up meetings for us with Dr Carlton Turner—who was President Reagan's director of the government's drug treatment programme—and with other leading figures in the armed services (where there was a worrying drug problem), and in the Food and Drug Administration, the government department which had the authority to approve all new forms of drugs and medical devices.

There was real interest at this high level, for many of the officials in the National Institute on Drug Abuse and in the Food and Drug Administration remembered me from the time of the previous administration under President Carter. It was also of great interest to George and me to find out from Herb that at least three out of the four top people we met were active Christians, so they were not only interested in the detoxification aspects of NET but also the spiritual rehabilitation which we considered so essential in the true cure of the drug problem.

By the end of 1982 Herman had produced a revised model of my device in cooperation with me; or, at least, with a measure of cooperation from me. He was still reluctant to concede that he and his chosen 'expert'—another one—needed any advice from me, or from Walter. In addition to his overt chauvinism, it baffled him, and all the other self-convinced experts in engineering and electronics he brought in, why it should be so difficult to produce a copy of my previous model of medical stimulator, with all my new ideas and technology incorporated in it.

Everyone involved, from the engineers to the financiers to the patent lawyers, were convinced that it would only take a couple of weeks to make a copy—and especially the Japanese when they realised its commercial potential—yet, as had been demonstrated with my earlier Model V attempted by Herman and his retired expert, in nine months they had come up with a flop, mainly because they were still unwilling to work with Walter's suggestions. The difficulty lay in knowing the relationship between the biochemistry of the body, the mysteries of the body's electromagnetic mechanisms, and the complexities of the effects of synthetic chemical substances in addictive conditions.

The Model VI produced by Herman and his new expert was technically much more complex than Model V, because of my involvement in the development process. But it was an unending battle trying to get information and cooperation from Herman. I have no doubt that he meant it for the best—he had no confidence in either George's or my own commercial or financial abilities—and so he excluded us from all the technical discussions. As he said to George: 'I wouldn't have the first idea about how to write a book or produce a film, so you don't know anything about organising and financing a multinational business project.'

But when I tested the new model on myself first, as I had done with all my earlier models, and then on a selected number of patients supervised by American medical colleagues as required by US official regulations, I found that, while it was an advance on my previous models in several respects, it was still far from satisfactory. Also, because I was reluctant to release all my information (even to Herman I had only given the basic minimum required to deliver an opiate treatment programme, and withheld the rest), I concluded that if the current model was not satisfactory for what I considered the simplest NET treatment process, it was unlikely to meet the more complex requirements of the other programmes still to be introduced.

But Herman overrode my strong objections, insisting that there was enough of an improvement to simplify its use for the medical profession. Also, he said that 'sixty per cent efficiency is enough when there is no competition in the market', and that we must push ahead urgently with production before any rivals came on the scene. I could have an improved machine in a couple of years. So he set up a company called NET Incorporated and started discussing participation with financiers.

We were not happy with the arrangements regarding this company when he informed us, and when we saw the terms he had for us we rejected them angrily and refused to sign the documents. Up to this time it had not been necessary for us to have a lawyer to represent our interests—and, also, we did not have the money to hire one—but now that contracts were being discussed we required one urgently. Herman had our power of attorney to use his 'best interests' on our behalf and, despite his stubbornness, he had done so after his eccentric fashion. However, we were increasingly concerned with the amount of influence that Herman's lawyer had over his decisions, and we had no confidence in him.

We discussed the situation with our pastor friend, Ben Patterson, with whom we had developed a close friendship, and he asked a lawyer member of his congregation, Bob Fry, to act on our behalf. When Bob tried to get information from Herman's lawyer he found him evasive to the point of rudeness, until George confronted Herman and demanded that he cooperate with our lawyer.

We were in an extremely difficult situation because we

were dependent on Herman paying the rent of our apartment, and our frugal living expenses. He claimed he was acting on our behalf, and that he wanted no part of the proposed corporation he was setting up to make the NET machines available world-wide. While we accepted Herman's assurances, we were highly suspicious of the manner in which he was depending on his lawyer, who acted as if he was ensuring that Herman was having a major participation in the proposed corporation. And, in fact, to our increasing frustration, when any interested financiers did enter into negotiations, the discussions always broke down because of the unacceptable participation demanded by Herman's lawyer.

Meanwhile, back in London we had worrying family problems. Myrrh had returned from her Far East sabbatical, and had begun her studies at the City University on banking and international finance (to have one member of the family who knew something about finance in the situation which was emerging), and she had telephoned to say that our bank manager—who had been so patient, understanding and cooperative over the years—had been told by his head office that we would have to take immediate steps to reduce our overdraft drastically, at this stage about ten thousand pounds. Also, she mentioned that she had not been keeping too well for several months.

I was very concerned, and I insisted on her giving me a detailed report from her doctor, from which I diagnosed that she had infectious mononucleosis, or glandular fever; a condition that usually dragged on for up to two years during which the sufferer had a variety of debilitating illnesses. At the same time I learned that Sean, who was still bicycling sixteen miles a day to and from the Imperial College of Science, in London University, had been knocked down several times by careless drivers; and as he was now about to sit his final examinations he was trying to find suitable but cheap accommodation nearer the college.

George's brother, Bill, and sister, Margaret, helped out

with our finances by providing the bank with satisfactory guarantees, so that took the weight off our minds. But we were in despair at not being able to help either Myrrh or Sean. They were both calm about the circumstances, and even urged us not to worry; but it put additional pressure on us to try and speed up a financial arrangement which would help us sort out all the problems.

About the middle of July, 1983, I had a telephone call from New York, from someone who introduced himself as 'the Chief Rabbi of Bethlehem'. He said that he had been impressed by my treatment because the son of a friend had been 'partly cured' by a claimed copy of my machine. He said he was the head of the Israel Torah Research Institute (ITRI), and that he was in charge of, or associated with, other organisations with millions of dollars in hand which could be used to bring my treatment to the poor of the world. He said he did not need to raise money like others who had approached us, because he already had all the money required. He would fly immediately to California and wished to meet urgently with me and my associates to discuss possible cooperation.

We met the Rabbi on July 19, 1983, with Herman and his lawyer; and with our lawyer, Bob Fry, representing our interests. Also present was Milton Freeman, who was a proposed director of the NET corporation Herman was continuing to set up without our permission. At this meeting our lawyer, Bob Fry, became convinced that Herman's lawyer was making the critical decisions—and that they were not in our interests.

The Rabbi was impatient with the delays in the talks and gave Herman an ultimatum of twenty-four hours to make up his mind. He showed to Milton Freeman an audited financial statement indicating that earlier that year ITRI was worth US$50 million, and he wanted to get the NET project moving immediately. The talks stalled when Herman and his lawyer demanded more than the US$2–3 million 'for the Kingsley group' being offered by the Rabbi.

This was the first we had heard of any payments being made at all, as Herman had said from the start that his services were being offered on the ground of friendship and that he had more than enough of his own money.

George abruptly told Herman that we were withdrawing our power of attorney, as we had not given his lawyer any authority to make decisions on our behalf, and it appeared to us that he was presently doing this—to our detriment. George, after consulting with Bob Fry, said he would put that in writing to Herman the following day. From now on we would make our own decisions.

The Rabbi was anxious for George and me to leave the next morning with him for Houston, in Texas, where he had several colleagues who were Christians and who were anxiously waiting to be associated with us in the project. They already 'had a clinic' and some staff, he claimed, and all it needed was my approval to get started.

We were met at the Houston airport by one of the Rabbi's Christian colleagues, Jack Cooper, with whom we were to stay in Houston. On the way home from the airport we were agreeably surprised to find that Jack and some of his evangelical Christian colleagues had been associated with the Rabbi in an oil project in Israel for the past year or more. He spoke highly of the Rabbi, and of his influential contacts in the Israeli Government; and told us that both the Rabbi and the Israeli Government had a percentage of their corporation in Israel. When we arrived at his home he showed us some of the impressive documents of his business involvements with the Rabbi.

This helped to allay our suspicions when we learned after a few days in Houston that there really was no clinic, and the so-called 'staff' were professionally unreliable and medically unacceptable to me. At the Rabbi's request, I had already sent to England for one of my senior nurses, Margaret Ellis, to join me in Houston, and we agreed to treat some patients as demonstrations of the NET programme. Margaret Ellis was unhappy with the Rabbi, his lawyer, and the arrangements he tried to discuss with her which, she said, were ethically unacceptable. Also, we could not get the Rabbi's lawyer to produce a promised contract, while he was urgently pushing me for all my 'evidence' regarding the credibility of NeuroElectric Therapy.

The patients whom we treated in Houston responded like all the others, exceptionally well, and the Rabbi and his lawyer were anxious to proceed with the establishing of a commercial relationship between us. However, despite the fact that they could fly in their lawyers and public relations advisers from Washington, they were reluctant or unable to come up with anything in writing—other than their initial letter of interest provided for Bob Fry before we left California. Bob had warned me not to make any move until I had something in writing, and not to sign anything until he had seen it and approved it.

With circumstances apparently proceeding so quickly we decided that we must return to England as soon as possible to sort out the problems of accommodation for our children, and our own finances. So we agreed that George should leave me in Houston to carry on the talks, while he returned to California to pack our few belongings (we had come to America with only the suitcase we had when we left Broadhurst over two years before!) and make preparations to leave for London.

I would go on to Washington with Milton Freeman (a member of Herman's proposed NET corporation, which we still had not approved, and which was under threat of extinction now that the Rabbi was interested in taking over) to advise me, when the Rabbi went there after a few days for the proposed meetings with government officials. It seemed that Milt Freeman was also cutting off his contacts with Herman and the NET corporation, but he assured me that he was continuing to act in my best interests because of the importance of what I was trying to do. Before leaving, George warned me not to sign anything—no matter who proposed it.

George had no sooner left Houston, when, sometime after dinner the following evening, the Rabbi called me to a meeting at his lawyer's home. I was driven there by Jack Cooper, whom we had come to like very much indeed, and Milt Freeman. We had to wait till eleven p.m. for the Rabbi's lawyer to arrive, and then he produced the draft of an agreement for me to sign, which he insisted I do right away. I protested at the timing and circumstances, and said that anyway I would have to consult George and my lawyer. But the Rabbi and his lawyer said they needed the document to take with them to Washington the next day, because they had made arrangements with high-ranking government officials in order to get their help in having NET approved urgently. I told them that I was already known to high government officials, and did not need any of their lower-level contacts.

Finally, after I continued to object strenuously, the Rabbi said to me, 'Meg, don't you trust me? I am a man of God.' (I had a passing thought of what would have happened if George had been present and he had said that to George, who had a low opinion of anybody who *claimed* to be 'a man of God'. I could hear his voice saying cynically: 'A sure sign that the man's a crook.') I repeated that I had been told to sign nothing, that it was late, I was tired, and I needed proper advice. The Rabbi and his lawyer then said they would tear up the document later if there was anything that did not meet with the approval of George or my lawyer; and that there were two witnesses—Jack Cooper and Milt Freeman—to confirm that assurance. So I signed. A decision that I was to regret deeply for the next several years.

We returned to London in August of 1983, and the Rabbi said that he would join us there in a few days. He asked us to arrange cheap accommodation for him at the same place as ours, saying that he would pay all bills and clear our bank overdraft as soon as he arrived in London. But he was mysteriously delayed in Washington, and our financial situation grew rapidly worse as we were presented with bills we had no means of paying.

Then, in the middle of one night, we were awakened by a telephone call from the United States. George took the call and I was vaguely aware that he was totally confused. Finally, he handed me the telephone, and it took me several minutes to understand that the caller was an irate father who was angry with me because I was charging him US$350,000 to treat his drug addict son! The father—who was a well-known millionaire—had put several lawyers and employees to finding where I was so that he could tell me personally what he thought of me! After some time protesting and talking to an eventually mollified father, it transpired that he was known to the Rabbi and had been told by him that 'Dr Patterson would treat his son with NET on condition that he paid this sum as a tax-free donation' to the Rabbi.

When I telephoned the Rabbi next day he said he was handling the money side, and to leave it to him. But then I had another call from the United States, this time from a young engineer in New York, who claimed that the Rabbi and his lawyer were demanding US$25,000 from him for treatment by me—although he had adequate insurance cover—also to be paid as a tax-free donation to an obscure charity. The young engineer went on to say that he was even more suspicious when he had checked out the charity, and had taped his conversations with the Rabbi and his lawyer, and that these were available to me if I wanted to take action against them.

Then I heard from Margaret Ellis, my nurse who had stayed on in the United States, that there had been another serious incident involving the use of my name by the Rabbi. He must have learned about my earlier contacts with Dave Crosby of the 'Crosby, Stills and Nash' rock music group, for he had arranged 'for Dr Patterson to treat him'. However, it appeared that he had admitted Dave Crosby to a motel and brought in some doctor whose name was also Margaret and represented her to Crosby as being Dr Patterson. Using the machine I had left with him, they had attempted to 'treat' him. According to Margaret Ellis, it had been a fiasco from start to finish, with the deceived Dave Crosby, suffering from withdrawals, chasing the terrified Rabbi down the corridors of the motel with a gun! Later, in his autobiography, Dave Crosby implied that 'a Scottish woman scientist' had treated him—although I was three thousand miles away at the time, knew nothing of the arrangement, and he was 'treated' by impostors.

When the Rabbi eventually arrived in London two weeks later he tried to slip away unnoticed from the small hotel he had asked us to arrange for him, where we were staying, without paying his or our bills. By chance we caught him as he and some of his friends were getting into a taxi to go to a nearby top-class hotel off Piccadilly. He was obviously disconcerted by our sudden appearance, and he quickly agreed to a meeting later that day with a friend advising us. He also said he would be producing a new agreement to replace the one signed in Houston.

When he did meet with us he was very aggressive, to the point of being personally insulting. He belligerently threatened to sue us if we 'tried to get out of our Houston agreement'. He shrugged off our accusation that two of the five cheques he had given to us in America, drawn on a Bank in Israel, had not been honoured. He denied that he had ever agreed to clear our overdraft at the bank—although we had witnesses to prove he had said this and we had it in writing in his letter of intent. When our friend pointed out to him that the Houston agreement had already been breached by him on several points, he became even more abusive and said that if I refused to work with him he would see to it that I got no more work anywhere in any part of the world for the next twelve years stipulated in the Houston agreement. Also, he would sue me for US$200,000 for breach of contract.

It was the beginning of a nightmare experience for me, and for the family. The Rabbi met with Pete Townshend and tried to get him to work with him, and when Pete refused he threatened to sue Pete. He even had his London lawyer put this in a letter to Pete, which Pete's own lawyers had to take seriously. So all the plans that Pete and I had previously made to start up a clinic in London had to be abandoned.

The Rabbi also used my name to approach well-known friends of mine, taking their names from the material I had provided him, claiming to represent me in my work, while raising money for his own schemes. He also approached some former colleagues and persuaded them to join him in an alternative scheme, where they would claim to be the true developers of NET and not me. Two of them were from the 'core group' in Broadhurst Manor who had been fired by us for making false statements, including a doctor who, according to someone who was present at the time, claimed he had 'treated eighty drug addicts by NET'— although, in fact, he had already left the clinic before we had admitted our first patient! These two were professing Christians!

Worse still, the Rabbi walked out of the Houston 'clinic' project, leaving Jack Cooper and his associates deeply in debt created by the Rabbi, and eventually bankrupting Jack. He then went on to involve other well-known but unsuspecting doctors and scientists in his schemes, still using my NET treatment material, but establishing it as his own under new names such as 'Lifenet'. We found out all about this when Milt Freeman, who had joined the Rabbi in his schemes, was also finally disillusioned and broke with him— deeply in debt because the Rabbi had 'borrowed' money from him and refused to repay him—and had drawn up a notarised list of the Rabbi's duplicitous dealings that he knew about, in order to sue him, copies of which were sent to us. We were unable to take any action against the Rabbi ourselves because, we were informed, it would take an expensive court case to free me legally from the Texas-signed document, and we had no money.

For several months we moved from house to house—family and friends—often sleeping on the floor, as we struggled to keep the NET project going. Eventually an unknown benefactor paid the rent of a small flat in central London—Lorne made it a condition that we did not ask who had given it but we have always suspected it was Pete Townshend—and we began to put the strands of our shattered life together again. But most of the donations we raised were still for NET research, and did not include living or travel expenses, so it was a battle to make ends meet.

In the meantime, I was having recurrent attacks of cholecystitis due to gallstones and it became necessary to remove my gallbladder. I dreaded this—it was to be my seventh major abdominal operation since my marriage in 1953, and every one seemed worse than the last. I am allergic to opioids, and after every operation (except for my three Caesareans, when no opioid could be given beforehand in order not to depress the baby's respiration) I would vomit continuously and require an intravenous drip for three or four days. However, a doctor friend recommended a Christian senior consultant surgeon from one of London's teaching hospitals, and he arranged to treat me in a private hospital. He assured me when I told him about my allergy to pethidine that he would tell the anaesthetist to give me only atropine before the operation so I would not be sick.

But when the atropine injection arrived it contained the usual pethidine. I objected, stating that the surgeon had assured me that no pethidine would be given; but the anaesthetist only declared 'it has to be given for a gallbladder operation'. I totally disagreed with this, having removed many gallbladders myself, but it was already too late to do anything but submit.

The result was that I was retching violently even before the operation began; and then, when I began to come round from the operation, I had the terrifying experience of vomiting again before I was able to move, with the additional agonising pain of a fresh wound. Mercifully, Myrrh was allowed to sit with me till I had fully recovered consciousness.

With the surgeon's permission, she attached my NET machine to electrodes on each side of the wound and I had no pain there. The only painkillers I had after the operation were two aspirins, and no sleeping pills at all.

On the seventh day the surgeon said I could go home. 'But,' I said to him, 'how can I go home with this constant ache in my side, running a low fever, and with a pulse rate in the region of 120 per minute?'

'That will all clear up by itself,' he replied. 'Come back and see me in six weeks.'

Afterwards, incredibly, the ward sister told me the surgeon had asked *her* why she thought I had this rapid pulse. But the surgeon himself never examined me to find out the cause.

Two days later I was sent home, very nauseated and unable to swallow anything but fluids. I was not very conscious of what was happening over the next several days, and only learned of the events later from George. For the first day or two he said little about my distress, assuming that I knew what was best for myself. Then, when my symptoms got worse he took it on himself to telephone the surgeon at the hospital to ask his advice. He was told the surgeon was busy and would call back later. When he did not call that day George telephoned the hospital the following morning. He was told the surgeon had not arrived yet, but would call as soon as he got in. He did not. When George telephoned later that day, he had already left the hospital. Next morning when he telephoned—my condition was causing George real worry, now that he saw I was beyond doing anything for myself—he was told the surgeon had gone on holiday, and that there was no replacement who could advise him.

By this time George was very angry, but despite demanding to talk with anyone who could give appropriate medical advice he was unable to do so. Finally, he began telephoning local doctors to see if anyone would pay a house call in an emergency; and after being refused several times, he found a newly qualified young woman doctor who agreed to come immediately. As soon as she examined me she said I had to be admitted to a National Health Service Hospital for urgent emergency treatment as I was in a very serious condition.

The senior surgeon in that hospital came immediately after my admission to examine me, and right away demonstrated to his junior staff a large swelling on my right loin, due to a collection of fluid which had been left behind during my operation and which was the cause of my severe toxicity. Turning to me the surgeon said the fluid would have to be drained within the next forty-eight hours. Later screening by CAT scan confirmed the presence of two large collections of fluid in the area of my recent operation.

By this time I felt so ill that I thought I might not recover. Despite my apathy I was conscious of an overwhelming sense of disappointment that I could not fulfil my vision for NET. This only intensified my deteriorating condition. Then I realised that God could easily replace me with someone else to complete what I believed was essentially His work. Dimly I accepted that, and lay back in peace to accept whatever God had in His plan for me.

The following morning I had a final screening before being taken to the operating theatre for drainage of the fluid. When the radiologist doing the screening had completed her examination, and she was reporting the results to the surgeon, I overheard her tell him that one collection of fluid had disappeared, and the other had become minute in size. The surgeon cancelled the operation and had me returned to the ward. At lunch time I ate a large plate of fish and chips—my first meal for three weeks. Later, the surgeon told me he could not understand what had happened. I could only assume God wanted me to learn yet another lesson.

I rapidly recovered, but as I started to pick up the

threads of the NET project again it looked as if I would never be able to get out from under the Rabbi's intimidatory threats to all who were interested in supporting my work. However, Christian friends of my sister, Edith, who heard of my predicament, offered to pay the US legal fees involved in getting rid of the Rabbi's false claims. They also persuaded their lawyer-cousin, Tom Washburne—who was a senior associate in a prestigious Washington group of lawyers—to represent me in the US court action against the Rabbi.

On June 5 1986—almost three years after meeting the Rabbi—we were successful in our court action against him when the Washington Federal Court Judge declared, 'All contracts now existing between the plaintiff (myself) and defendants . . . are declared to be null and void *ab initio* from their inception and any rights or obligations alleged to be flowing from such contract or as a result of any such contract are likewise null and void.'

At the time, however—even as the court case was proceeding—the Rabbi, while stating in his deposition that he had not set up any research centres or places to use the NET treatment process, was seeking to enlist the services of a scientist, Dr Bob Beck, (in Dr Beck's telephoned statement to me, 'to help develop Dr Patterson's machine'). The Rabbi also told Dr Beck that he had obtained the services of Dr Christian Barnard, the famous South African heart transplant surgeon, to 'develop an electrical stimulator to treat drug addictions'. This was confirmed by Dr Barnard himself in a reported interview in the *Baltimore Sun*, where he said: 'I'm working with a group of researchers in London, Houston and Los Angeles, who are involved with the possibility that by stimulating the brain you develop a technique whereby you can withdraw people from drugs.'

- 12 -
Taking the NET Treatment to the World

$\mathcal{D}$uring the professional hiatus caused in our life by the activities of the Rabbi, George and I had devoted ourselves to research and the preparation of material for publication. In a sense, it could be said that what the Rabbi had intended for evil had turned out to be for our good in that the enforced withdrawal from all public use and talk regarding NET forced me to use the time in investigations that I would normally have postponed until a much later date. The same was true of George, and both of us had prepared an enormous amount of material ready for use when we were free to do so.

But, meanwhile, other people had got on the electro-stimulation bandwagon and there were several electronic stimulators being put on the market in the United States and the United Kingdom purporting to be 'derived from the black box used to cure famous rock stars'. When these were brought to my attention, and I had investigated them, I found that they were really only variations on the Transcutaneous Electrical Nerve Stimulator (TENS) devices being used for some time to treat chronic pain, but their claims were based on my published writings. Like the early Chinese pulse generator which I started with, these had currents and frequencies and wave-forms which were within the parameters of certain drug signals (as we had found in Hong Kong with heroin) but were totally unreliable from the point of view of adequately treating addictions. Their signals were only rough approximations, and it was usually only a case of luck rather than good judgement when they chanced to hit the signal required for any specific drug. In other words, they were where I had begun some sixteen years before, and they had a long way and much research to go to produce a device which would be officially approved. So we were not unduly worried.

But Herman Kingsley had also set up an operation in California to exploit his version of NET. Without saying anything to me he advertised in leading US newspapers that his company, NET Inc., was selling distributorships across the country. In the material he sent to interested parties (who forwarded copies to me because they thought I was part of the operation) he included, without saying anything to George or me, private correspondence between Dr Winston, Dr Becker, the well-known expert in applied bioelectricity, and myself, as well as other confidential material we had given him. Some of the people associated with him claimed that they 'had raised thirteen million dollars' to facilitate the project. When George wrote to Herman on several occasions asking for an explanation, he was provided with none, only short replies wishing us well.

I had no fear of either Herman or the Rabbi as competitors, for I knew the machines they were working on were limited in performance, as they included only minimal information on one drug, and inadequate without skilled supervision (demonstrated by the Rabbi's attempt to treat Dave Crosby, as recorded in Crosby's autobiography), which only my trained, experienced staff could provide—and none of them were prepared to work for the Rabbi or Herman. They had made the fundamental mistake of only consulting electronics experts, with no specialist doctors in the field of addictions, so they knew nothing of the bioelectronic treatment process. Also, the machines they had were based on outdated material, and had been bypassed by my new model, on which I had been working during my Rabbi-enforced 'wilderness exile'.

The same was true of even lesser operations with grandiose claims, such as one group set up in the United States by a doctor and an estate agent. After using— unattributed—information about the history of neuro- electrical stimulation, and its uses in England and Hong Kong, the company made claims that are suspiciously akin to what I have published. In their literature the doctor (whose name is unknown in the field of electrical stimulation) and the estate agent claim their device is their 'brainchild' derived from their—so far professionally unpublished— experience.

Despite the pressures and distractions caused by the Rabbi's activities, I discovered through an American friend that the Rabbi—in flagrant disregard of the court order which had instructed him and his lawyers to hand over to me all the confidential material he had obtained from me—had instead sold it through his Lifenet companies to a leading California corporation. When I tried to get information from the Californian corporation they did not return my calls or reply to my letters. When I made enquiries I discovered that, despite their claims, they had not submitted their device, obtained from the Rabbi, to FDA for approval.

However, George and I planned to return to the United States to set up double-blind clinical trials as required by the Food and Drug Administration, and to launch the NET project. In our previous discussions with the US govern- ment officials, we had found that, despite the publicity for media and public consumption, they were as uninformed and uninterested regarding the real solution to the drug problem as the authorities in Britain. What activities there were had been directed towards the law enforcement agencies, and cosmetic education programmes, with little or nothing for innovative research and treatment. But there were private individuals and foundations who were interested in doing something to find solutions.

In Britain we had found that the government and media were more interested in accepting the opinions of the medical establishment—the same people who had been so unsuccessful in finding solutions for so long—than in exploring possible new solutions.   The advisers to the government on addictions were psychiatrists, and the contributors to discussions of the problem on the media were psychiatrists.   I, as a former surgeon, suffered from the prejudices of both psychiatrists and government officials.

I learned that when the government—the Department of Health and Social Security—was approached by enquirers asking about my NET treatment they were sent a copy of an article printed in the *British Journal of Psychiatry* about a research experiment conducted at the Maudsley Hospital, London, 'into the effects of NET'. Despite the fact that this was a poorly constructed methodology, with only eight cases completing the trial, with claimed 'NET advisers' who were, respectively, a commercial salesman and a minimally trained nurse, and improper use of 'NET', this was presented by the government officials as definitive.   Even when I protested, and sent a photocopy of a later letter I had published in the *British Journal of Psychiatry* repudiating the Maudsley research study on almost all points, the DHSS officials continued issuing the totally misleading report.

On the other hand, to my knowledge, they have never sent anyone a copy of any of my publications. Yet the Maudsley report itself admitted 'the subjects [on NET] . . . showed a more rapid improvement' than those on methadone (the standard government-approved treatment).

Just as we were arranging to leave once more for the United States in 1986, I was approached by the family of a famous rock star, Boy George, to treat him for drug addiction.   Details of his dangerously acute problem had been lead items in the media for days, and I was reluctant to get involved in such circumstances. I wanted to get away from treating privileged individuals and get on with launching enough NET stimulators so that the national and international problems of addiction could be at least mitigated; and internationally all addicts would have treatment and possible cure available to them.

The chief problem in dealing with internationally famous rock star patients—more than any other form of entertainers—with a few happy exceptions, is their inflated, even grandiose, ideas of their own importance. They don't see themselves as sick people needing to be cured; but as special people doing the doctor a favour by allowing him or her to treat them. They think they are not really sick, just unfortunate victims of an occupational hazard; and the doctor is the fortunate choice to be elected to join them in the subsequent media extravaganza. Finally, if or when they do recover, this is usually claimed to be self-accomplished by exercise of until then hidden but innate self-insight and self-will, without any assistance from the doctor.

In my experience of treating a large number of them, only a few—such as Pete Townshend—were able or willing to rise above this ridiculous arrogance. When the condition was drug addiction, and a necessary part of the treatment was to confront the addict with the need to change current values—or lack of them—for a more stable and healthy belief system in their own long-term interest, their reaction was almost comical with outrage. Were they not writing songs about social evils and high aspirations, with millions of people approving their compositions and performances by buying their records?

However, Boy George's condition was so critical that I agreed to treat him, but under strict conditions of secrecy because I had heard of his passion for publicity. He has since talked at great length to the media about his addiction, giving different versions I have noted, so this account is not a breach of medical ethics. It has the added advantage— unlike his own account—of being witnessed by other observers and participants at all times.

I arranged with his record producer, Richard Branson, to treat Boy George at Richard's home in the country, away from the attentions of the demanding media, with my senior assistant, my son, Lorne. Lorne had been my most experienced colleague for most of the other rock stars I had treated. When we disappeared from London, the media continued to print fallacious stories, including descriptions of the 'clinic' where he was supposedly being treated—one said to be in London, one in Northampton, and one even in the United States, all nonsense.

George and Sean went off to the United States as we had planned earlier, and Myrrh had already gone there for a holiday on the completion of her degree at university. Lorne and I arranged to join them in about ten days.

It was absolute pandemonium. The international, as well as national, media were now covering the Boy George story, joined by the police who were searching for him because of the publicity about his blatant drug-taking. The politicians were hounding the police and magistrates to ensure that Boy George was not given any favoured treatment because of his glamorised reputation.

The police arrested Boy George's brother for heroin possession, searched George's various homes for signs of drugs, and announced that he was wanted for questioning. I agreed with Richard Branson that he should let the police know where we were, and that we would present Boy George to them at the end of his treatment, and this proposal was agreed by the police.

Eventually our location at Richard Branson's Oxford home was discovered by the media, and car-loads of journalists mounted a 24-hour watch around the estate. Some even got inside the grounds and attempted to take photographs through the windows, until we had to draw all blinds and close the windows. It was impossible to treat him in such circumstances, and we slipped away one evening, after dark, through the fields at the rear of the house. I was wearing only open sandals, and the fields were filled with thorns and thistles, so Richard insisted I ride on his back! We went by prearranged car to another 'safe house' but several of Boy George's friends found out and visited him there, and proper treatment was no longer possible.

However, the morning after the move, for some reason—probably the mounting political pressures—without waiting as they had agreed, and halfway through his treatment, police arrived to take him away to a London police station for questioning.

I was extremely angry, and let the police know. As was my usual practice I had stopped all drugs on admission, and now I had to remove my NET stimulator from Boy George at a critical stage of treatment on the fifth day. I demanded that Lorne and I accompany Boy George to the police station, as he was still under our medical care and responsibility. The police were obstructive, but I was furious, and persisted, and eventually they agreed.

We were in police custody for over ten hours, with Boy George becoming increasingly distressed as the effects of NET diminished without the stimulator. His withdrawal symptoms began to reappear under the pressures of detention and questioning by the police. It appeared the police had been unable to find any signs of drugs in their investigations, and they were determined to get their 'proof' by forcing an admission through self-incrimination under pressure from lack of drugs and lack of treatment.

I protested strongly at these police tactics with a suffering patient, and eventually I was able to persuade them to permit Boy George to have the NET stimulator attached—which quickly reduced his tensions, and the withdrawal symptoms disappeared. Except for the period of interrogation Lorne and I were now allowed to stay with Boy George, and he recovered dramatically. It was an impromptu demonstration of the efficacy of the NET treatment in difficult circumstances, before sceptical and unsympathetic police witnesses. I wanted the police to record an official statement of my protest at their conduct, but they refused—although they did take advantage of my being present to claim to the media that my presence indicated their treatment of Boy George was 'humane'!

When Boy George's treatment was completed a few

days later I agreed to appear on television to denounce the police strategy of arresting and charging an addict solely on the basis of his applying for medical treatment for addiction, with no supporting evidence whatever; and of making this the basis of an official charge against a patient. I had met a high-ranking police official and he had confirmed to me that the police actions were totally unacceptable and should never have been permitted by their superiors. This episode, however, resulted in many patients being afraid to request treatment in case that gave the police licence to charge them with possession of drugs. It was a disgrace to both the police concerned and the judicial process which condoned it.

Ironically, the politicians who had been the cause of the injustice in the first place, and the media who had been so hypocritical throughout, now expressed 'outrage' only at the small fine imposed on Boy George, instead of attacking the travesty of justice. He was happy with the amount of publicity generated then and later, and to get public sympathy grossly exaggerated what he had undergone in the treatment itself, ignoring the fact that he was under constant observation by a variety of witnesses at all times. It was not the NET treatment that was painful for him, but being confronted with the need for a different lifestyle which would include practising different values. The difference between Boy George and Pete Townshend in their responses to both the detoxification and the rehabilitation aspects of their treatment was an interesting reflection of the difference in their characters.

All of this meant that my planned visit to the United States had to be considerably curtailed for, immediately on arrival there, I was caught up in a series of media interviews because of the international Boy George interest. It was a further distraction from my search for a high-technology company with the expertise to make the fifty prototypes of my new Model VII MEGANET stimulator. This was even more technically advanced than the Model VI Herman Kingsley had been unsuccessfully trying to produce, and I

had tried to find a suitably equipped company in Britain—
even in the new regional areas of electronics expertise—but
had been unable to do so.

The return to the United States to find a company was
tinged with a feeling of trepidation because of my earlier
experiences. How was I going to find my way through the
jungle of commercial and financial wild animals waiting to
pounce on my potentially profitable device? I did not object
to their making money; but I did object to their making
money for themselves at the expense of the sick and the poor.

Lorne and I had just arrived in Vermont, where George
was on holiday with Sean and Myrrh and the Winston
family, when George told me that Joe Winston junior
wanted to have a private talk with him. Afterwards, George
refused to tell me what had been discussed, saying that Joe
wished to keep it secret until he mentioned it. That same
afternoon George and I took one of the boats out into a
maze of waterways in the centre of the lake and were on our
way back when we passed Joe and Myrrh in another boat
just going out. Two hours later they returned, late for the
evening meal, and Myrrh came over to me at the table
holding out her hand—it showed an engagement ring! She
told us the story while Joe grinned.

When Joe had asked her to go boating it raised no
suspicion, as the various members of the family went out
sailing, boating, fishing and water-skiing with each other at
different times. In the maze of waterways Joe had suggested
pulling into one of the small islands, and after wandering
around Joe began throwing stones in the water. Myrrh was
casually watching when he said, 'Isn't that a bottle in the
water?' and she said, 'Yes, and it has something inside it.'

Joe inveigled Myrrh into fetching it out of the water,
and after she had retrieved it, she said excitedly, 'It is an old
paper with a message on it.' When she tried to open the
bottle it was sealed, but being curious like her mother she
opened it anyway. The bottle contained a conch shell and a
piece of rolled parchment. She took out the parchment, and

it was a love sonnet by Shakespeare. When she had finished reading it, she turned the bottle over to see if there were any clues as to its sender. She then noticed that there was a diamond ring hidden in the curve of the shell. At this point Myrrh had her first suspicion. She couldn't look up at the smiling Joe until he said, 'Will you marry me?'

Joe had been planning to propose to her for several weeks, without saying anything to Myrrh or anyone, until he had asked George for his permission and blessing to marry her. Although she would not admit it until afterwards, she had been in love with him since she was twelve years old, but he had never shown any interest other than that of a good friend. He had never kissed her nor even held her hand until one week beforehand, so his expression of love was as much a surprise to her as it was to us.

Joe junior was a computer engineer and, while I was discussing with him the problem of how best to go about finding a high-technology company who could produce my prototypes, he said that he worked with a research and development company which was fully equipped to do the work I described. He arranged for me to meet Art Beard, the president of Formation Incorporated, after the holiday.

My meeting with Art Beard was satisfying beyond all my expectations. He called in all his company experts, and, after a sustained discussion it was agreed they could, and would, produce the fifty prototypes that I required for the clinical trials necessary for official approval by the Food and Drug Administration in the United States. They calculated it would take nine months to complete and test them.

But they also said that it would probably cost around $195,000—and that was after Art Beard generously offered not to charge anything for the labour involved! So, once again I had to look for research money. And once again, this was provided mostly by our good friends Pete Townshend of 'The Who', and Ron Frates, the chairman of the Frontiers of Science Foundation in Oklahoma City, with some donations by grateful patients.

In the event, it took eighteen months and cost almost
$500,000 (not including living or travel expenses) to produce
the fifty prototypes of the MEGANET Research Model VII,
automated and pre-programmed, which could be used by
anyone without the long training necessary with my previous
models. The delays were caused by the unexpected
technological problems involved, but the superb team of
experts at Formation Inc. solved every problem, and Art
Beard carried all the extra costs.

Art urged me to exactly copy, in so far as possible, the
parameters of my Model IV stimulator with which those
trained in its use had been able to treat the various
addictions so successfully for over ten years. When the trial
breadboard of the new computerised model was ready for
me to test on myself, the highly skilled engineering staff of
Formation Inc. were insulted and furious as I told them it
was no good. 'This woman, who is merely a doctor . . .' they
raged—or so I was told at a much later date.

However, they listened to me. For several days, I sat at
their workbench with their breadboard attached to
electrodes behind my ears and, literally hundreds of times,
they made some tiny change in the shape of the wave till I
affirmed repeatedly (by mutual agreement, I was not
allowed to see the shape of the wave on the oscilloscope)
that one particular shape was what I required. Unknown to
me, they repeated that one shape over and over again, and
were astonished to find that I unfailingly approved one
particular shape and—mildly or strongly—rejected every
other shape they tried.

Over the years, I had studied many of the theories
regarding the shape of a signal—slow rise, rapid rise, and so
on—but now I was claiming to know what was acceptable
without even seeing the shape of the wave. I still do not
understand this, unless it emerged from a specific intuition
such as I had noticed in my surgical career, of being able to
diagnose accurately the cause of an 'acute (emergency)
abdominal condition' before any investigations were done,

based only on my informed diagnostic intuition.

My final choice was justified in the next few years, when all my special nursing staff agreed that, with the Model VII, the NET treatment was more rapidly effective than ever before.

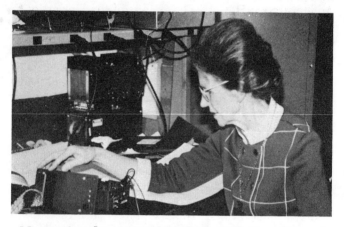

Meg testing the MEGANET VII in the laboratories of Formation Inc.
1987

With that problem overcome I could now devote myself to the last major hurdle—the organising of the double-blind clinical trials at accredited drug treatment units attached to leading universities, which would provide me with the required material for submission to the Food and Drug Administration for their official approval. I knew from my discussions with them in the past, and again more recently, that—despite all the claims being made in the media—no one had come to them with a medical device for drug and alcohol detoxification for their approval. If I could push ahead quickly now, my stimulator would still be the first, and the most important. Also, I had no fear of taking responsibility for developing the device over the years, while all the other imitators would have problems finding someone of sufficient reputation and credibility in the medical field to do this.

The clinical trials were arranged, and conducted independently in two reputable centres: the Veterans' Administration Hospital Drug Units of the University of Pennsylvania, in Philadelphia, and New York University Medical Centre. The Pennsylvania University trial was conducted by Drs Charles O'Brien and Tom McLellan; and the New York trial by Dr Richard Resnick; all of them with high reputations in the drug treatment and research fields. Dr Resnick had previously expressed extreme scepticism when interviewed about NET, saying, 'I could get the same results by using chicken soup!' However, he had kept in touch with me, and was keen to conduct the trial in New York. Within a short time of starting to use NET, he publicly renounced his statement of previous years, and stated that NET was not a placebo effect.

In New York, the nursing and counselling staff of the Veterans' Administration Hospital showed such resistance to the extra work involved, that the study there had to be dropped. On the other hand, the Philadelphia VA staff were very research-oriented and all gave superb cooperation after Lorne treated five of their most difficult drug addict patients as a demonstration of its efficacy, in a pilot study. The physicians there—despite, or perhaps because of, their previous scepticism—confessed to being deeply impressed by the preliminary responses, when the stimulators were used by themselves in their independent studies, without my being present. They have concluded that NET effects have been shown to be clinically, although not yet statistically, significant.

However, to my dismay I discovered after two years of research that if I submitted the findings based on my Research Model VII to the FDA of the US Government, approval would cover only this particular model and not one for commercial distribution. This meant that I would have to find another $500,000 for a new simplified design which could be easily used and sold world-wide.

During the time I was pursuing the clinical trials in the USA, I was also making plans to introduce the treatment into all the countries which had continued to express an interest over the years—even Britain, where there was little or no evidence of interest! However, as the time for launching the treatment world-wide drew closer, the difficulties involved in such a vast commercial enterprise grew greater.

While the prototypes were being made in the USA I continued to seek financial support for the commercial model and to set up a clinic, such as we had had at Broadhurst Manor, in Britain and in the United States. Time after time we entered into discussions with individuals or companies or finance groups expressing keen interest, followed by more detailed negotiations, and these would fall through when it came to the small print of the contracts. Either the people concerned had no money themselves but were going to raise it on the strength of my medical device and reputation, or they had the money but wanted to control its medical development (for example, its financial potential in obesity, rather than the treatment of the paralysis diseases I wanted to research), or they wanted all the profits with insufficient built-in safeguards or commitments for me to pursue further research. The talks all fell through, and I became increasingly despairing.

Among other interested people I met in the USA was Charles 'Chuck' Colson. Chuck had been the legal counsel to President Nixon at the time of the Watergate affair, and had been imprisoned for his part in it. While in prison he had been converted (which he has described in his book, *Born Again*), and because of what he had seen and experienced in prison he had set up an international organisation, International Prison Fellowship, to work among prisoners. We had since met on several occasions to discuss how best my work could be used to help the prisoners in Chuck's work. He was also interested in helping me to make NET available to others as well as prisoners.

Throughout all these developments George was writing books which could be used for the rehabilitation treatment following on the NET detoxification. The first of these was already published, entitled *The Power Factor*; and the second, *The Paradise Factor*, was scheduled to be published in 1994; but it would take some time for the others to be ready for publication and bring in any adequate income. Consequently, we were in even greater debt than we had been at the time of the Rabbi's activities, and were only able to continue because the Bank of Scotland manager was very sympathetic to our plight and cause, and two American family friends continued to pay the rent of our flat. We had to scramble around for the remainder of our living expenses in an embarrassing, even humiliating, way.

While I was arranging this, George was approached by a leading film company to act as their consultant in making a major film about Tibet. It was the same people who had made the award-winning *Chariots of Fire*, *The Mission*, *The Killing Fields*, and others—one of them George's former colleague on the *Raid into Tibet* TV film, Chris Menges, who had won an Oscar for his camera-work in *The Mission*. George was reluctant to do so at first, mainly because of our commitments to the drug problem, but was eventually persuaded to agree. He left for Tibet once again in 1988, this time openly and not secretly, with two noted producers and a scriptwriter. The visit had a traumatic effect on him when he saw the horrendous damage done to the country and people by the Chinese Communists. On his return to London he sat down and poured out his feelings in a new book about Tibet—an expanded sequel to his earlier book, *God's Fool*—entitled *Requiem for Tibet*.

He was writing this when I, with Lorne, had to leave for the United States yet again, to arrange the final phase of the clinical trials—still without any financial support. To keep the costs down to the minimum we borrowed our daughter's car—a small red Honda two-seater sports model—and drove the six thousand miles from the east coast to the west coast and back again as we set up trials in different places, and held discussions with interested entrepreneurs of various kinds.

Through Art Beard, president of Formation, I was introduced to Ross Perot, the noted American entrepreneur, who had built up a multibillion-dollar enterprise, and he expressed interest in forming a joint venture with me in making NET available world-wide. But, once again, when it came to the small print, my lawyers in America and England would not permit me to sign because it was not in my personal or professional interests to do so.

We had several other similar experiences—all of which proved unproductive, either because the interested parties had insufficient capital to launch the project, or our lawyers in UK or the USA would not give their approval to the proposals.

All I could do was struggle on with the fund-raising, the research and the promising clinical trials. To satisfy the FDA authorities I also had to provide, in addition to my own work, a personal analysis of all work being currently conducted world-wide in the field of electrostimulation.

I also accepted a long-standing invitation to visit the Soviet Union in 1989, with my son Lorne (who was now my research coordinator), to discuss NET. While in the Soviet Union I had two major engagements: one was a special lecture at the famous Moscow Serbsky Institute of Psychiatry (where, just two weeks before, a delegation of USA psychiatrists visited to decide if they would allow Soviets to become members of the International Association of Psychiatrists again, from which their membership had been withdrawn because of their treatment of dissidents in that very Institute—readmission was refused). My lecture was attended by staff members of the Institute and by senior members of staff in charge of the various Moscow hospitals involved with drug and alcohol addiction. After a one-hour lecture, it was thrown open for questions, and after fifty minutes of non-stop questions, the meeting had to be reluctantly brought to a close. The interest was demonstrably intense.

This was followed by an International Symposium on New Approaches to the Treatment of Alcoholism and Drug Dependency—the first ever in the USSR to include any mention of drug addiction. It was held in Gagry, in Georgia, and attendance by international experts was by invitation only. In addition to representatives from the Communist bloc of nations there were senior delegates from the West. There were fifteen leading drug and alcohol specialists from the USA, two from Canada, one from France, and Lorne and I were the sole representatives from Britain. Another significant factor was that the Soviet Union had just entered into an agreement with the USA for an exchange programme of specialists to share their findings, with each country sending a representative for six months.

The Symposium was opened with a welcome banquet given by Professors Ivanets and Anokhina who headed up all the addiction research in the USSR, and Dr Gela Lezhava, Head of the Scientific Narcology Centre for Georgia, in Tbilisi (the place of the recent major demonstrations). The food was sumptuous, new dishes were brought in continuously, the caviar and vodka were of the highest quality and toasts went back and forth throughout the meal. My toast to two minority groups, the Scots and the ladies, went down well. But even better was Lorne—dressed in his kilt—telling a Scottish joke as the evening got merrier. He was not only a superb ambassador for NET, but also a wonderful travel-companion!

After giving my lecture, I was invited officially to enter into an agreement of cooperation with the All-Union Research Centre on Medico-Biological Problems of Narcology of the USSR Ministry of Health. They were intensely interested in NET, and my MEGANET Research Model VII stimulator was far in advance of anything that they were using in their own experiments. I said I would be delighted to cooperate.

The Symposium closed three days later with an hour of open discussion and comments. The *only* individual talk mentioned was mine, and two people spoke in appreciation of my work—Professor Borodkin of Leningrad and Professor Anokhina, Deputy Director of Narcology for the entire USSR.

Returning to Moscow, Lorne and I explored their highly efficient new Metro, whose stations resemble art galleries, and crowned our stay in Moscow with a visit to the brilliant, fascinating Moscow Circus, a permanent institution with nightly performances. We then took the overnight train from Moscow to Leningrad, an eight-hour journey. It was cleaner and more efficient than British train travel, and obviously something in which they took great pride. We were wakened half an hour before arrival in Leningrad with light classical music, and the guard brought us large glass mugs, in handled pewter holders, of delicious black tea out of the traditional samovars.

Although met by Intourist, we chose to spend our four-day visit totally on our own and had no problems doing so. The hotel was modern, located in a beautiful forest of silver birch. Only the wooden dachas of the favoured officials were nearby. And taxis into town were cheap.

After exploring the Russian Museum (hundreds of paintings by all the great Russian artists), we had difficulty finding a taxi back to the hotel, because apparently taxis were only allowed to pick up at certain places. Eventually, seeing our predicament, a Russian lady from Armenia helped us—she spoke a little English. She shared a taxi with us and invited us to her home for 'a cup of tea'. Instead, she gave us a full meal!

That evening we managed to get tickets for the only ballet available during our stay. The large Kirov ballet was sold out, but we got a box in the smaller Maloshoi theatre—and that for only £9 each. The ballet was French (Putin) and based on *The Hunchback of Nôtre Dame*. The ballerinas were absolutely superb. It was a *wonderful* Russian performance.

The other memorable experience was a morning spent at Petrodvorets, on the shores of the Baltic Sea, thirty kilometres from the centre of Leningrad. It was the palace built by Peter the Great in European style, the large gardens dotted with fountains and statues. It was destroyed in the Second World War when the Germans besieged Leningrad (but never defeated it) for 900 days. The buildings were reduced to a mere shell, but have been lovingly and painstakingly restored from 1944 onwards, and they have tried to make it an exact replica of how it was in Peter's day. It never ceased to amaze us that what seems on the surface to be such a dull, practical Communist society has been putting so much money and effort into bringing back the beauty of old Russia.

The taxi-driver who took us back to the hotel refused to take any payment at all. He said, 'Leningrad is my city and I am just happy that you have enjoyed it'!

The Russian people's hospitality was most considerate and generous. We even appreciated all those fearsome *babushka* guardians of public places, cloakrooms, museums, etc., who, on seeing the hopelessly lost and confused stranger in their midst, without exception offered the comfort of their maternal wings.

On my return to Britain from Russia I was due to visit West Germany where one of the leading medical groups wanted to set up a series of clinical trials such as I was just completing in the United States. There were about twenty or thirty countries in other parts of the world where I had either visited, or who had corresponded with me and invited me to visit and demonstrate NET to them, and we were now almost ready to move ahead.

Ironically, in Britain in the spring of 1990 Mrs Thatcher's government was arranging an international drug conference to which I was not even invited. In 1988 one of

her Cabinet officials, David Mellor, had paid a highly
publicised visit to the United States, seeking information on
how best to deal with Britain's drug problem. He was
followed a year later by another cabinet official, David
Waddington, also seeking at first hand how the United
States was attacking its increasingly critical drug problem.
At the same time the leading US experts in the drug field
were clamouring for information about 'Dr Meg Patterson's
NET treatment' from my colleagues in Philadelphia and
New York, and the US media were reporting the dramatic
successes!

The wilful obtuseness of government and medical
officials had ceased to surprise me, however. I pushed ahead
with preparing the material for the clinical trials,
supplemented by studies by other authorities in the field of
electrostimulation. I also began making research notes on
the next stage of my studies into the effects of electrostimulation in the degenerative and paralysis diseases.

Our younger son, Sean, was now working on nerve
regeneration, with the intention of sometime in the near
future investigating the effects of NET on such a process.
He was later to receive a grant from the American Paralysis
Association for this purpose. He had graduated Ph.D. in
Cambridge University, to add to his B.Sc.(Hons) from
London University. His studies were in the field of
molecular neurobiology, with special emphasis on pain
mechanisms, and he had obtained a prestigious NATO grant
to pursue postgraduate studies at Stanford University,
California, into nerve regeneration with particular
application in the degenerative diseases such as Parkinson's
disease—the field I hoped to enter when I had handed over
my addiction work to an assistant. In the introduction to his
doctoral thesis I was deeply moved to read his inscription:
'This thesis is dedicated to my parents who taught me

patience and sound judgement, and the value of seeing things through.' It made all our difficulties over the years fade into insignificance.

Our eldest son, Lorne, was supervising the clinical trials and laying the foundation for future expansion of NET. Myrrh had graduated in banking and international finance, with honours, and was advising us on the financial proposals we were facing almost every month or so. Joe, her husband, had provided me with technical possibilities that were even beyond what I had conceived, in the Research Model VII, and was considering the design of a commercial MegaNET. And we were grandparents now, as Joe and Myrrh had a daughter of their own, Aisling.

George was having several books published, and having discussions with Hollywood's Orion Pictures Corporation, regarding a film of his involvement with Tibet based on his new autobiographical book.

While everything was going well with the arrangements for clinical trials in the United States we were facing the worst crisis of our lives. The advance royalties from the various books were swallowed up immediately by the demands of my own and my team's travel expenses to and in the USA for the supervision of the clinical trials. For the sake of advancing NET, all of us lived frugally. We had finally reached the end of the road as far as money was concerned.

I was due to return to the United States in late May of 1990 where Myrrh was expecting the birth of her second baby. George and I had just been to Scotland to attend the wedding of one of my nephews when, two days before our arranged departure for the United States, George suddenly took ill and it was discovered he had had a 'silent heart attack'. The doctors refused to allow him to leave the country with me, and although I was going to cancel my visit to the United States, George insisted that I must go to be with Myrrh for the birth of the baby.

In the event, when George had completed his tests it was found that there was only damage to one vessel in the heart, and he was permitted to travel for two months to see if the condition would be helped with medication and rest. A decision whether to operate would be taken on his return to London.

Two weeks later Myrrh had her baby—a second grand-daughter for us, Arianne—and George was able to join us, before travelling on to Canada to participate in an important conference and seminar at Regent College in Vancouver, on the subject of 'The Past, Present and Future of the Christian Brethren Movement'.

While he was there I was invited to visit Texas to discuss possible cooperation with the president of a small but reputable firm making CES medical stimulators for the treatment of stress and anxiety. The firm was Neuro Systems Incorporated, and the president, Ray Gilmer. Our son-in-law Joe Winston went with me to advise me, and we were very impressed during our visit—so much so that we arranged another visit, this time in New Jersey with our younger son Sean, as well as Joe, to discuss seriously the possibility of a joint venture in North America and world-wide.

Like us, Ray Gilmer had been struggling for many years to consolidate his company's work and had just reached a significant point of breakthrough. He had known of my work for several years but this was the first opportunity we had had to meet and discuss mutual interests and plans. It was a true meeting of minds and our family were united in the decision to link up with Ray and Neuro Systems. Ray was poised to expand rapidly in the United States, and was currently having discussions with important Russians in the academic and commercial world regarding joint ventures internationally. Some of the Russians he had been talking with were doctors and scientists I had also met during our visit to Russia, so there was an exciting overlap of interests. Together we made a formidable team at the highest level of the new field of electromedicine internationally.

Unfortunately, Ray's reach was to exceed his grasp. Just when it looked as if we were going to be successful in setting up an international corporation together, Neuro Systems lost several major customers because of cutbacks in insurance payments to health centres, and the company was rendered financially unstable. With twenty-four hours' notice, I was informed that they were preparing to declare bankruptcy.

At that time, we had wound up the lease of our apartment in London, had once again got rid of accumulated possessions to the Salvation Army and Oxfam, and had transferred our most important materials—books, research papers, some clothing—to the United States! Before they arrived in Dallas, Texas, we were left without financial support and home—again.

However, in the several months of our association with Neuro Systems we had met a number of influential people in the United States who were interested in my work, and also the work of Professor Lebedev of Leningrad, with whom I was working in Dallas. Funds were found to make it possible for him, before he had to return to Russia, to complete the research he had begun at the Universities of Texas and Toronto, enabling him to ascertain for the first time exactly where the electrical current affected different parts of the brain when it was applied externally.

My senior assistants, our son Lorne and Noel Flood, had already visited Germany in the summer of 1991, and arranged a series of treatment demonstrations there prior to launching NET in Germany, to be expanded later into Europe. They did likewise with our Russian colleagues in

Leningrad, now renamed St Petersburg, with a view to introducing the treatment into Russia.

With the bankruptcy of Neuro Systems, once again we had to start looking for immediate funding in order to design and complete a commercial Model VIII version of the successful MEGANET Research Model VII. But economic crisis had seized the United States and research funds were being severely restricted.

In August 1991, family and relatives gathered in central Ireland for the marriage of Lorne to Beatrice, a bonny Irish lass, who was Noel Flood's sister. Before the wedding, we held in-depth discussions about the future of NET, and Joe and Myrrh decided that our only hope was to put all the money they had saved to buy a home into designing and making this commercial Model VIII. With two children and a third on the way, and living in a small house, this was an incredibly brave decision. It meant that Joe would need to do all the work in his spare time, in addition to a job that often required overtime. But they were convinced this was what God wanted of them, and they were fortunate to have a close friend for a partner, Dave Meyers, a skilled young businessman, who was likewise looking for God's way for him and his wife. They agreed to handle all the business complexities and paperwork. It was a superb combination, and we set up our own company InterDigitation Inc. to manufacture the device. Later we set up our distributing company in Scotland, called NeuroElectric Therapy (NET) Ltd.

The first unit Joe designed was Model 802 MegaNET stimulator, a simple-to-use 'Jeep' version of the complex research Model VII, designed specifically for simplified application in all addiction treatments. The planned second unit, the MicroNET, even simpler to operate, was being designed for at-home stress management, after detoxification.

As we go to print, the first fifty units of Model 802 are ready for Germany and we are in the process of organising a world-wide programme for the treatment of drug, alcohol and cigarette addictions. We are also using the same or similar exciting developments in bioelectricity by other recognised international experts to address other major intractable medical conditions by these new and much less physiologically dangerous treatment processes.

It is now over forty years since George and I first met on the Himalayan border, in Kalimpong (and we calculated on our fortieth wedding anniversary on September 12, 1993, that we had moved house some forty-six times during that period) and we were over seventy years of age. Like Abraham we were still pilgrims moving on, looking for a city and a country promised by God.

In 1952 we had thought we could not get married because of the apparently irreconcilable vocations of our lives. At that time, we had gone ahead to an unknown future with God. Now, not only the two of us, but our whole family, have been brought into a glorious venture with God that no one in their wildest imagination could have foreseen.

As I close this story of my life I am reminded of the lines by the poet, Bertha Gernaux Woods:

Counting their lives not dear, so they discover
    Some bit of truth through eons all unguessed,
Something to make the lives to come the richer,
    Ere they themselves shall shut their eyes and rest.

Ah, still the Lord God walks with noiseless footfall,
    Visits the workshops of these patient men—
Smiles on the test tubes, the revealing lenses,
    And 'It is good,' he murmurs once again.

George and Meg's 40th wedding anniversary and
Sean's 32nd birthday, in Moorestown, New Jersey.
Back row: (left to right) Claudia Tomes (now Sean's
wife, an Argentinian scientist), Sean, Lorne,
Beatrice (Lorne's wife, who is Irish),
Myrrh, Joe Winston (Myrrh's husband).
2nd row: Arianne Winston (3), Aisling Winston (5).
3rd row: George with Helena Winston (16 months)
and Meg with Tara Patterson (Lorne and
Beatrice's daughter, 9 months).
12th September 1993

Epilogue

With the publication of this book, and the completion of the commercial Model 802 MegaNET stimulator in the United States, in 1993, we were also ready with the other books prepared during the enforced period of professional silence.

Because we agreed with the 19-country Council of Europe's (Strasbourg, 1970) report on the drug problem (namely, that 'there is something very wrong with society . . . the problem is one of a whole society and an entire lifestyle shared by young and old alike') it had seemed necessary to us that we should address not only the fundamental addiction problem of detoxification in my NeuroElectric Therapy researches, but also what is wrong with the whole society. The Council of Europe had defined this, to a degree: ' . . . this subject includes not only psychological and medical but also social, educational, cultural and political aspects.'

The failure of psychiatrists to deal with the problem was rooted in their professional inability to address the basic *spiritual* factors involved in the complex nature of addiction. (It is estimated that over 50 per cent of psychiatrists are atheists or agnostics.) And the failure of the ecclesiastics to deal with the problem was rooted in their professional inability to address the basic *political* and *social* factors. Between them they had left a vacuum in their respective countries which was making the cure of the problem impossible.

It is this gap which we are trying to fill with the publication of the material which we have prepared. Because our own beliefs are rooted in the Judaeo-Christian principles outlined in the Old and New Testaments of the Bible, our proposals are based unapologetically on Scriptural models rather than the failed Greek myths of the psychiatrists (for example, the incident where we informed the psychiatrist that we had taken our rehabilitation treatment of his patient from the parable of the Prodigal Son, or Loving Father, in the Gospel of Luke, chapter 15).

With this as our guideline we have jointly written two books to encapsulate our combined approach to the solving of the world-wide problem of addiction:

The Power Factor: This deals with the basic problem of all addicts: 'I am not able to . . .' It also categorically opposes the popular concept of some treatment processes: 'Once an addict, always an addict', or 'Never touch another drop', or 'I *am* an alcoholic.' The Scriptural principle is: 'God did not give us the spirit of timidity, but the spirit of *power*, and love, and *self-discipline*.'

The Paradise Factor: This deals with the acknowledged but rarely dealt-with problem of 'the pleasure principle' in addictions. How do you replace the 'dream of Paradise' which is the synthetic experience of every addict, and which also lies deep in the heart of every individual?

These books are the products of our personal and professional lifetime's experiences. In addition, there is my up-graded (4th edition) medical/scientific book about NET, entitled, *The Addicted: The Revolutionary NeuroElectric Therapy*, which includes the most up-to-date findings from my researches in clinical trials; and an *NET Treatment Manual* describing the practical and technical applications, compiled by Lorne and his colleague Noel Flood. We hope that these, used in conjunction with my new Model 802 MegaNET stimulator, will make a revolutionary contribution to solving the world's drug and alcohol problems.

Index